THE RIVER IN SUMMER

MAURY M. HARAWAY

authorHOUSE®

AuthorHouse™
1663 Liberty Drive
Bloomington, IN 47403
www.authorhouse.com
Phone: 1-800-839-8640

Published by AuthorHouse 1/9/2013

ISBN: 978-1-4817-0495-3 (sc)
ISBN: 978-1-4817-0494-6 (e)

"Eternity is in love with the productions of time."

William Blake

Preface.

We live our lives in the changing seasons of the Earth around us. Members of our species once were alert to every nuance of change in their surroundings. Their survival depended on it, and this was still true up until a few hundred years ago. We were profoundly influenced by every season and every weather. But we made many discoveries and inventions that gradually gave us the appearance of lessening our dependence on the natural world that surrounds us. First we tamed fire, bringing our own light and warmth to the night. Fire brought comfort, but maybe almost as important, it brought security by keeping predators away from the camp or cave. Later, much later, we got candles, then whale oil lamps, then kerosene. Now, for a while, we have had electricity, providing heating and air conditioning and operation of a wide array of invented devices to keep us entertained and allow us to work or play throughout whatever hours we please.

How different it is when the power goes off! Consider not only the power gone but all batteries, all generators, and all devices dependent upon them. We've only gone back about a dozen decades. But our lights are gone, to be replaced by candles. Our television is gone, our computers won't work. There's no telephone. We are hard pressed to cook our food. Our refrigerated and frozen supplies are gone. The power that draws our water is gone. We can't get a drink. We can't even flush the commodes. What a difference with a mere loss of electric power! We have come a long way, indeed, from the majority of our experience as a species.

In this book I wish to turn my focus back to the natural environment that is our heritage and to the changing experiences that come with each season of the year. I want to look closely at the world in which our lives takes place, and to whose history we contribute.

Because the seasons flow one to another without pause, seemingly forever, we might pick any starting point we wish to begin the story. The tide of life never ceases, has no beginning or ending that we can imagine. To us it might as well be eternal, a continuing bounty going forward in beauty. Let us see if we can take a look at that beauty.

We are accustomed to a starting point for the year we have accepted for so long that it seems natural to us. It is the time we celebrate as New Year's Day—what we boldly take as the beginning of a new year. Its location was not chosen at random, and not exactly with reference to the seasons, either; for, in truth, it is located near the middle of winter. New Year's Day, like the official schedule of the seasons, was not located according to variations of weather or of the seasonal activities of plants and animals. Rather these focal points of our calendar were chosen in reference to celestial events that never fail or vary.

The official beginning of winter is set at the occurrence of the shortest day of the year in what we call the Northern Hemisphere of the Earth, where the people who established the calendar we use lived. Up until that date (December 21), for six months, each day has become progressively shorter than the one before. After that date, the length of each day begins to grow progressively with the approach of spring.

Consider for a moment what a massive event the solstice must have been to primitive peoples. For months, the Sun was receding with each passing day, receding, going away, perhaps never to return—the Sun, on which all life on Earth depends. But on that momentous day, the Sun began to return, growing stronger day by day until it prompted a rebirth of plant and animal life.

No wonder, then, the Winter Solstice became the most important time of celebration in the year—the day the Sun came back, the day life began to grow again! No wonder it is at this time that we celebrate the birth of Jesus, and a few days later, the birth of a new year. Here comes the Sun! "Happy New Year," we shout. The expression of the Japanese on this day conveys its significance even more plainly. "Happy spring," they shout! Yes, happy spring! Here comes the Sun!

Winter to Spring.

A New Year.

The sun rises clear and brilliant in the cold air of mid-winter, spurring life in semi-dormant trees and stirring the animals of the day to action. We call this the opening day of a new year. In the yard around the house, a robin greets the new year with the caroling song of spring. His song matches the full sunshine but not the temperature, which stands at twenty-four degrees. Here at mid-winter, the robin's song anticipates the spring, when his ability to perform it will determine the quality of the breeding territory he will be able to hold, the mate he will be able to attract, the start in life he can provide to his progeny.

It is a morning of heavy frost, yet many local animals are vocal and active in the first hour of daylight. A gray squirrel performs his territorial song nearby. It is none too musical, perhaps, but he sings it vigorously, maybe even proudly. His singing has a more timely connection with the season than the robin's song, for January is one of two major annual breeding times for squirrels, and the more vigorous and assertive males in an area will account for most of the breeding done there, at least on the male side of things. His song asserts his boldness, his health and vigor.

Squirrel pups conceived now will be born in mid-spring, in coordination with an explosion of plant growth, a swelling of flower buds, and an inception of new seeds. Those conceived in the year's second major breeding season will be born in early autumn, in time for the fall ripening of nuts and seeds. The major breeding times of squirrels allow for the offspring produced to be born at major times of richness in the food supply. Actually, squirrel courtship can occur successfully at all points between January and July; pups born of breedings that occur between those two major breeding times must emerge into the richness of summer, and so should still do okay.

Other birds are singing in the cold air and bright light. At least two of the small, gray, tufted birds called titmice repeat their clear whistles from separate locations, each proclaiming its own territory for the coming breeding season. The loudness of their songs contrasts with their small size. A cardinal—my grandmother called it simply a redbird—performs one of his standard song elements, but it represents only a small portion of the rich and varied repertoire he will display in coming weeks.

Besides the robin that is caroling, many others are performing extended chirping calls that approach songlike complexity. Red-bellied woodpeckers are sounding their barking calls and a few of their more musical notes. Blue jays are making their loud *jay* calls and one other of their impressive menu of sounds—a high-pitched, musical tinkle. A few large blackbirds are in the vicinity, restricting their comments to a few flat-sounding chips. These grackles, too, possess an impressive array of vocalizations, most of them raucous and only slightly musical, but often pleasing to the ear—at least to my ear.

The resident mockingbird of the dooryard sits in his favorite perch in the walnut tree near the back door of the house, quietly surveying his domain. He will remain unobtrusive unless a robin or other interloper appears near his food supply: For example, the red berries of the holly bushes. He keeps his one-acre territory the year round, and with the onset of spring, proclaims his ownership with a prodigious outpouring of song. For now, he is mostly silent.

I will share the adventures of this year with Cathy, as I have shared those of many years before. Her name is Catherine Gail. She was Cathy to her schoolmates and friends, and that is what I usually call her. Sometimes I call her Catherine, as her sisters still do and her parents always did. She is my wife and the apple of my eye. She retains the athletic body and a good deal of the attitude of the tom-boy she was as a young girl. Maybe you will recall the actress Audrey Hepburn as she descended the stairs of Professor Higgins' home to attend the royal ball in the film *My Fair Lady*. That is the way Cathy looked as a young woman—the way she still looks, in an appropriately mature version. There is a stream outside the town of Natchez called Saint Catherine Creek. I've crossed it many times, each time taking pleasure at the name.

In the bright afternoon of New Year's Day, Cathy and I drive sixty miles south toward the old town of Oxford, first crossing the Coldwater River, then the Tallahatchie. The valley of the Coldwater is a mile wide across the flat bottom surrounding the river; the valley of the Tallahatchie is twice that width. Both river bottoms are covered with thick growths of lowland hardwoods and cypress timber that form wildlife corridors many dozens of miles in length. Plenty of wild mammals here: Raccoons, river otters, 'possums, mink, muskrat, beaver, bobcat, coyote, gray fox, deer, squirrels, rabbits, skunks, and various rats and mice. There are almost no bears anymore, no wolves, no panthers. Only their names survive: Bear-tail Bottom, Panther Mound, Wolf River.

Plenty of fish here, too: Largemouth bass, crappie, three-and-a half-foot gar, seventy-pound catfish; bluegills and river pan-fish, three-and-a-half-inch darter minnows, six-inch black crayfish. These last are not fish but crustaceans, yet it seems proper to mention them among the water-breathing denizens of the river. There are myriad snakes and turtles and venerable species of water birds—great blue herons and great egrets, and in summer, little blue herons, green herons, and snowy egrets. There are crow-sized pileated woodpeckers, hawks, owls, vultures. There are wood ducks year-round and a variety of waterfowl in winter.

This part of the country is under high atmospheric pressure today—under one of those "Hi" symbols on the weather maps. The local consequences are that the sky is exceptionally blue and deep, clear and limpid; visual images of ordinary objects are projected in striking clarity and sharpness through the thin air of low humidity. The deep blue of the sky is enhanced by contrast with high, white cirrus clouds whose reflective qualities brighten the day. The combination of deep, bright sky and vivid images of the rugged hill country, with its covering of short-leaf pines, give a suggestion of the high country of the American West.

The cirrus clouds foretell an approaching cold front. If it brings moisture, or precipitation, it will be snow. Snowfall is a treat in North Mississippi. Not just children but almost everyone hopes for it, urges it on. But we don't usually get it.

As we pass through the wooded hills, I'm struck afresh by the beauty of sycamore trees. They are among the most impressive features of the forest at this time of year, when the leaves are gone and one can see deeply into the woods. They stand out, smooth of trunk and clean-limbed, and shine in the sunlight, white as bleached bone.

The sky was still bright as we made our way home. We saw a number of red-tailed hawks—one of our largest and most common hawks—and a single red-shouldered hawk. The red-shouldered hawk is slightly smaller and more slender than the red-tailed and favors a woodland habitat rather than open country. And we watched an American kestrel, our smallest falcon, dive from its perch on a power line, glide smoothly to the ground, and catch a small mouse in the talons of his left foot.

We had pan-broiled sirloin and home-fried potatoes for supper. And black-eyed peas, of course. If you live in the South and don't eat black-eyed peas on New Year's Day, you may as well hang it up.

January Freeze.

There's been a big freeze across the north half of the state. What was widespread water is now ice. Most of the ducks are gone from the delta, frozen out of here. In the white and frozen landscape the presence of any instance of wildlife is heightened, conveys an elemental significance.

> Among twenty snowy mountains,
> The only moving thing
> Was the eye of the blackbird.

> Wallace Stevens

Well out in the delta I find a large flock of white-fronted geese feeding in an open field not too far off the road. I stand watching in the frigid air as large groups of snow geese, hundreds of birds in each group, begin to funnel down from high in the sky to land and feed in the same field with the white-fronted geese. Drifting down from hundreds of feet up, slowly revolving in a huge spiral. Becoming a single massive group of three thousand snow geese. A look with binoculars as large numbers of geese come in to land or take off from a field provides an unforgettable view. Just hold the binoculars still as hundreds of closely packed geese drift through the range of your magnified vision. You won't soon grow tired of what you see.

> A thousand snow geese
> Steeply dropping in spiral
> In an iron-gray sky.

I went to look at a large reservoir built decades ago when the U. S. Corps of Engineers dammed the valley of the Coldwater River near the junction of the hills and the delta. A few hundred yards of free, unfrozen water remained in the miles long lake at the base of the dam. Five thousand ducks of various species were crowded together in that limited space. Among them I was astounded to estimate a count of twelve hundred hooded mergansers. The male of this species is quite handsome when he opens the crest on his head to reveal fully the brilliant black-and-white contrast of his hood. These birds are not particularly scarce, but one is always glad to find them. They are nearly always worth mentioning among the highlights of a day in the field. To see them in such numbers was unprecedented. The largest groups I could recall seeing in one place had numbered in the teens or low twenties. Here were twelve hundred—driven to this one spot of open water by the quick freeze across the landscape!

The Flight of a Falcon.

A medium-sized but powerful falcon, a merlin, flew with leisurely wingbeats low above the stubble of last summer's soybean field in the flat land bordering the Mississippi River. At a certain moment, it feinted sharply toward the ground, and at that instant a meadowlark took flight from the spot toward which the falcon had gestured. The falcon dived on it and caught it in its talons as smoothly and easily as a game of pitch and catch. The meadowlark's try for escape had failed, but it really had little chance once sighted by the falcon. If it had hunkered where it was, the falcon would simply have taken it from the ground rather than from the air. In one sense, the meadowlark continues its journey through the guts and tissues of the falcon—not so dismal a prospect, perhaps. In another sense, it simply returns to the sky of its birth.

Winter Feeders.

Early this morning I watched the fast-paced feeding of three tiny birds in the shrubs near the house. Yesterday afternoon I had seen a ruby-crowned kinglet and an orange-crowned warbler feeding there. This morning they were joined by a golden-crowned kinglet. The kinglets are closely related cousins, whereas the warbler comes of widely separated lineage. But all three make a living by feeding on small insects and spiders and the eggs of insects and spiders, and all three have evolved a common feeding technique and employ nearly identical patterns of movement. Their feeding includes numerous quick, short hops from leaf to leaf. Often a hop is accompanied by a few quick wingbeats, mere flicks of the wings. The wing-flicks sometimes flow smoothly into full hovering flight, usually maintained only for a second or two as the bird gleans an insect or an egg from a leaf. Sometimes they are able to perch briefly as they glean and so avoid the energy expenditure of hovering.

It is a pleasure to see their lively behavior on a cold morning, and impressive to consider that each arrived here after traveling all the way from breeding grounds near the northern border of the country or perhaps in Canada.

Courting Squirrels.

Two groups of three squirrels, each group in a different tree, chased one another around, running up and down and around the tree. One particular squirrel in each group was always in the lead. Another always maintained second place. And the third always hung back a little behind the first two. The leader seemed little concerned to escape its pursuers but often appeared to hold back the pace to let them catch up.

In my interpretation, the lead squirrel of each group was a female nearing a condition of reproductive receptivity, the individual immediately behind her was a dominant male, and the squirrel hanging behind a little was a sub-dominant male, staying too far away to provoke aggression from the dominant male while staying close enough to make an approach should the chance occur.

Blue Jay Talk.

Conversational interchanges among blue jays enliven the mornings of heavy frost. Their repertoire of calls is impressive. The *jay* call is so familiar that it might as well have served as the source of the blue jay's name. This one call is subject to much variation and is used in a wide range of circumstances, often being involved in flocking behavior, or the gathering of numerous individuals to a central location.

Another call reminds me of the two-note sound of a cuckoo clock. The first of the two notes is of higher pitch than the second. This call has been described as the most musical of the blue jay's sounds. They also perform a musical, high-pitched tinkling call comprised of three or more linked phrases.

Several of their calls are decidedly non-musical—a screechy whistle of several syllables at different pitches, often compared to the sound of a squeaky gate or an old, hand-operated pump; and a two-note whistle that sounds like a ricochet bullet in an old western movie, but quicker and softer. Jays are excellent mimics of the hunting calls of the red-shouldered hawk and the red-tailed hawk, as well as the broad-winged hawk. The red-shouldered imitation is the one I hear most often. It is a strident, two-note whistle, the first note of higher pitch than the second. Sometimes the imitation is close enough to the real call of the hawk to cause a human observer—at least this human observer—to question whether it was made by a hawk or a jay.

David Sibley says, in his *Guide to Birds*, that blue jays occasionally perform a soft, thrush-like song when on or near their nest. I recall hearing this song only once, when as a boy I climbed high in a tree and sat near a blue jay nest, watching the blue jay pair that were perched beside it.

To me, the jay's lack of a commonly heard song—despite their obvious vocal virtuosity—fits well with the fact that blue jays also are not notably territorial, and territorial defense is a widely recognized function of bird song. We are unable to ascribe precise meaning to any of the impressive variations of blue jay vocalization, but their breadth and frequent usage are testament to the richness of social life within the species.

Blackbird Alert.

A dusting of snow covers the grass and the fallen leaves like a super-heavy frost. One hundred and seventy-five big grackles settle into the trees near the house. Their vocalizations combine in a cacophony of sound. I step suddenly into view from the porch and there is an abrupt halt of their vocalization, creating by contrast a startling silence. I've often encountered the demonstration before but it has been a while since I considered its importance to the blackbirds. The sudden silence of a portion of the flock issues an effective warning to the entire group, who immediately join in the silence. The birds are now at full alert, and if a predator should attack at this time the swirling escape of one hundred plus grackles may lessen its prospects of snagging a member of the flock.

On the Bank of the Mississippi.

Cathy and I drive in early afternoon right to the edge of the Mississippi River twenty miles west of our home. We walk along the high bank, close enough to hear the rippling of the water and the wash of waves against the sandy edge. The first impression—the overwhelming impression—anytime you approach The River at close range, is of its immensity—the sheer volume of moving water, the incomprehensible almost incredible power of its massive current. It stretches three-quarters of a mile in width and five miles in length from a given point on its bank. You can't often see farther than five miles of its length from one spot because of its twisting turns across the landscape. Numerous eddies across the breadth of the current stand out visually as maverick ripples running contrarily to the general flow.

> Unstoppable flood
> Of a sprawling continent.
> Father of Waters!

The land stretches as flat alluvial soil for several miles on both sides of the river, here. At other places, as along old Front Street in Memphis, the river runs in close against the Chickasaw Bluff on the east bank, so that the bluff rises almost directly from the water.

Dozens of ring-billed gulls work the shoreline today, flying back and forth, upstream and down, their heads turning constantly as they watch the water, alert for a passing meal at the edge of the stream. They cry out to each other as they search. Big white puffs of cloud float as individual islands in the ethereal blue of the sky.

Much later, at sundown, the treetops of home are bathed in an eastern version of Rocky-Mountain alpenglow as cloud banks across The River on the western horizon reflect across the landscape the light of the setting sun.

Evening on the Gulf of Mexico.

Low-slanting sunlight strikes the far banks of Middle Lake in Gulf State Park, Alabama. Across the narrow strip of land to the south of camp the surf booms on an inland wind across the Gulf. The breaking clouds are elemental forces in the light of the evening sky. The sky and light behind an extending point on the southern shore, dark with pines and live oaks, are backdrops to the pale, bald tallow trees and tanned-out cattails that border the lake. I wish I could hold the scene, capture it all with a paint brush. I think of a line from Ian Tyson's song about the painter Charles M. Russell—that when Russell went to his "Home Up Yonder," the Lord told him "You're in charge of sunsets / In old Montana / 'Cause I can't paint them / Quite as good as you." Some of us might say, however, that when Russell painted, so did the Lord.

As daylight failed, a Cooper's Hawk—a bird killer—crossed the lake heading inland from the trees on the south shore. And just as full darkness descended a pair of woodcocks stepped out quickly from a thicket at the edge of camp and came out into the open grass to probe for worms with their long bills. They seemed to be having good luck with the worms because I was able to make out frequent moves of their heads and bills indicating capture and feeding. Within a minute of their arrival in the open the light had dimmed to the point that I could no longer make out any field marks on either bird—probably an important factor in the timing of their foray into the open, else some other predator might feed on them as they were feeding on the worms. Shortly after full dark one of the birds made a soft, twittering call, and a little later, the other did likewise.

Gannets.

In the afternoon we walked beside the surf at the Gulf of Mexico. The sand was well-packed and easier to walk than it sometimes is. The scene was enhanced beyond measure by the spectacular feeding of gannets. These large birds are often to be found only at sea, far out of sight of land. But in winter great numbers of them come close enough to the shores of Alabama and Florida that one has the opportunity to see them from dry land.

Gannets feed by soaring in large groups high above the surface of the sea and diving headfirst from the air to catch fish. The birds I watched soared at heights from twenty to seventy feet above the water, and many made dives from at least fifty feet high. They were feeding a quarter-mile or so out in the Gulf, but I could see them clearly without binoculars.

They must have been feeding on shoals of fish, because often when one bird dived to the surface it was followed immediately by another, then two more, three more, another and another, and so on. On one occasion I counted fourteen different dives in a continual series.

When a gannet spots a fish at a vulnerable depth (we must imagine the bird's actual experience, as it remains forever unobservable to us), the bird folds its wings partly in toward its sides and begins a steep, almost vertical dive all the way to the water. As it falls, however, the bird maintains enough wing surface against the air stream to allow quick adjustments to the movements of its target. In the last few feet of its dive, the bird must quickly throw its wings back directly to the rear in preparation for a high-speed entry into the water. It must do this perfectly on every dive of its life, from the first to the last. Else the collision of extended wings with water would break the wings and end the bird's career. Also, as it enters headfirst into the water it must catch and hold its prey between the mandibles of a bill that appears admirably designed for fish-catching.

Gannets have evolved bills that are notably similar to those of terns, kingfishers, loons, and herons. These groups of birds are widely separated from one another in genetic heritage. They may be no more closely kin than an elephant and a mouse. But they share a common functional characteristic in their dependence on catching fish. And this common functional necessity must have figured in the evolution of their bills.

Pelicans.

Two brown pelicans came gliding, soaring along ten feet above the water just out from the beach where waves were breaking. One made a dive headfirst vertically into the water, plunging its head well below the surface. As the first bird brought its head up from the dive and settled itself to float on the surface, its companion made a similar dive by its side. Both birds caught good-sized fish. They held most of the bill under water as they floated, taking twenty seconds or so to strain excess water from the inflated pouch in the lower mandible of the bill until not much was left there but the fish. Then they threw back their heads to swallow. You could see the outlines of the fish still in the pouch as they initiated the act of swallowing.

Both birds continued to float on the surface and continued to hunt as they floated. Each held its long neck in upright posture and tucked the head so that the eyes were directed at the water and the bill was held parallel to the extended neck. From that position they made quick stabs deep into the water, a considerable reach being provided by the long bill and long neck. Each bird caught several additional fish in this manner before first one then the other took flight again and went to rest at the top of a seawall nearby.

A good depth of water was running below the seawall through a channel connecting the sea to a fresh water lagoon that lay slightly inland. One of the pelicans moved up to the edge of the wall and began looking intently into the water, its feet poised at the edge of the wall as though ready to dive. Then it did dive, headfirst into the water. Bringing its head back above the surface, it held its bill partly submerged for a full minute as it strained water from its pouch. When it finally threw back its head to swallow, I could see it had caught even a larger fish than before. This one may have been a foot long.

High-tech Woodpecker.

A red-bellied woodpecker drummed against the metal gutter above our bedroom on the second floor at dawn, advertising his claim to the territory as breeding season nears. Usually woodpeckers content themselves with making a sounding board of a tree trunk or branch. The substitution of our gutter afforded this woodpecker a high-tech amplification of his usual message-strength.

The improvisation—call it spectacular adaptability—of birds is widely displayed to an honest observer. The phrase *bird brain* is an aphorism that reflects more harshly on the speaker than on the object of his derision.

Wise but Cautious.

Late in the day, after the blackbirds had cleaned out my bird feeders again, I refilled them to allow the cardinals, chickadees, and white-throated sparrows a few mouthfuls of feed in the closing light of day. As I filled the second feeder I noticed a male cardinal sitting in a tree nearby and apparently watching me. As I went back to the porch, the bird began an approach to the feeder, but was quite cautious about it. His first flight brought him within ten yards of the objective, but he took seven more perches, each closer than the last, before arriving on the feeder at the end of his ninth flight and the passage of about two minutes.

The Party Never Ends.

Seventy brown-headed cowbirds came crowding around our feeders. Two males sat near the top of a tree as a female perched on a branch just above them. One of the males simultaneously vocalized and performed his ruff-out display, extending the wings partially open and ruffling the feathers along his back, sides, and breast. The male beside him remained quiet and never bristled as his neighbor displayed. The dominant male performed more than a dozen displays, then flew to a different perch nearby. The female immediately followed him. They flew into the foliage of a dense cedar tree and out of my sight. I doubt that copulation occurred on this occasion—there are no nests to receive their eggs as yet—but the time is soon coming when there will be.

Cowbirds are parasitic nesters. The females must sneak about and lay their eggs in the nests of other species, where their young will be nurtured by the (unsuspecting) foster parents. It is thought this species-typical behavior of cowbirds evolved in accommodation to their affinity for following buffalo herds in their wanderings, always keeping with the herd and not taking time to stay in one place and raise a brood. But that greatly simplifies what must have been a complex process. At least one can imagine a situation, long in place, that gave selective advantage to cowbird mothers who left eggs in the nests of other species and then stayed on at the party, continued on their merry ways with the herd as it wandered, and left additional eggs in other birds' nests as they frolicked along.

Mockingbird Tour de Force.

Today at mid-morning our mockingbird began a singing performance that will continue, with brief interruptions, across the next five months. It will be one of the most impressive displays of animal behavior to be witnessed anywhere. As far as I can say, he is singing for the second time this year. Many weeks will pass before another day finds him silent. Everything in his life will now be defined by his songs. On his singing will depend his feeding and breeding territory, his mate and the well being of his family, and the demonstration of his iron will, his prowess, and his extreme vigor.

Information Learning.

This morning looking out the breakfast room window, I saw Mockingbird do something I took as remarkable. He had been sitting ten feet high in a walnut tree near the house. At a certain moment he jumped from his perch in a smooth glide that took him almost to the ground and straight under my fifth-wheel camper. He glided under more than ten feet of the camper's length, then soared up to a landing on the edge of a large planting pot well on the other side of the camper. The underside of the camper has only one foot of clearance above the ground, but Mockingbird sailed through the area and up to his perch on the other side without altering the smooth curve of his glide all the way from the tree to his landing on the pot.

The interesting thing about all this is that the underside of the camper and the pot on the other side of it could not have been visible from the perch where Mockingbird began his glide. I interpret the entire sequence as evidence that the bird had some sort of neural representation (perhaps also a mental representation) of the layout of this portion of his environment and that he made use of that information in launching and completing his glide. Such information could only have been acquired by the bird's previous experience in that familiar environment.

This view of learning and the performance of learned behavior—that animals acquire specific information about the environment from their experiences and act on that information in the performance of learned behavior—is a popular one in the current study of animal learning. This sort of interpretation was pioneered by the cognitive behaviorist E. C. Tolman, beginning in the late 1920's. The term *cognitive* refers to thought processes, or at the least, informational processes. These are not necessarily conscious or mental process, although Tolman didn't rule out that they might be. This theory describes how cognitive processes, themselves unobservable to us as they involve anyone but ourselves, might be related to the performance of observable behavior.

Of course, cognitive theory (information theory) is only one of a number of available interpretations of animal learning. The observation of Mockingbird's behavior this morning gives an example of why this sort of interpretation is popular among today's animal psychologists.

Surprise Snow.

What a surprise! On rising this morning I found the world utterly blanketed with six inches of snow—unpredicted as usual. Well, sometimes they predict it right, but just as often, it seems, the snow comes as a surprise. I guess it must be tricky to predict snow with accuracy in this part of the country. Even trickier than most weather predictions.

The day is overcast with cloud but still fairly bright, enhanced by reflection off the snow. Cathy and I put on our boots and go out in the four-wheel drive truck, set in four-wheel, high range. We can drive thirty miles an hour and hold a good grip on the road without straining the transmission. We drive all over the township, weaving to and fro from one side to the other and back again. The full blanket of snow is uniform everywhere.

There are no tracks but ours on some of the roads we take, and we see only a few people abroad. There are a couple of groups of children building snowmen in their yards and a couple of groups out with parents on hillsides to try some sledding. We see only a few birds out and no mammals but dogs. Even the red-tailed hawks are mostly taking the morning off from their usual watching posts.

We stop off at a grocery store on the way home and pick up a chuck roast and some potatoes, carrots, white peg corn, tomatoes, and onions so I can make up a batch of Jane's Vegetable Beef Soup when we get home. My mother made that soup every now and then throughout every winter, but she nearly always made it when we had snow. It's good to continue traditions, and the soup is particularly good with Cathy's exceptional corn bread. A black woman named Roxie (more about her later) used to cook for our family when I was a boy, and even now my brothers and I often measure the excellence of someone's cooking against what Roxie used to turn out. Cathy's cornbread is as good as I remember Roxie's as being.

Farewell to an Old Friend.

Today I visited again with an old friend on his death bed, where he has lain for the past three weeks. He was brother-in-law to my uncle, a close friend to my father and mother, and is as near an uncle to me as he is a friend. Chester came back a hero from the great World War II, with a bullet wound through the chest and a bronze star. I knew he had been a hero from the things my mother and father had said and from the sincerity of their feelings about his service. Chester himself always down-played his story anytime my brothers and I could get him to talk about it at all, but a time or two he let us look at and feel the large scar near the center of his upper back that was left by the exit wound.

He has been reduced now by illness almost as much as a man can be reduced and still live. Yet we had a good and pleasant visit. He was not absorbed at all with his own predicament and hardly seemed to take any notice of it.

We spoke of how much my parents had meant to both of us and of what good friends they had been to him all his life. I told him it made me happy to see him but I hated to see him having such a hard time. "Oh," he said, "it's not so bad as that. I'm getting along all right." Toward the end of my visit I said he'd been given a hard hand to play but was making a good job of it. "No, this isn't so hard," he said, "I'm not doing much."

Rivers of Birds.

From now through to full springtime waves of birds flow across the sweep of the land. Large flocks of robins, blackbirds, cowbirds, and waxwings pour across our skies and into our fields and neighborhoods. Robins in the hundreds often occupy large sections of this old residential neighborhood, especially in the early mornings, as the onset of spring varies with the continuation of winter in mid-February.

After a cold December we have had a very mild January, and the elm trees and the daffodils flowered a good two weeks earlier than usual. This mild weather has continued through most of February. Robins that will breed locally already have established pair bonds for the season and are in the process of establishing territories. You see them patrolling, male and female together, on the alert for worms and insects and showing mild hostility toward others of their species who approach them.

Close-packed flights of cedar waxwings buzz through the skies and swarm as one into treetops and into holly bushes, where they feast on red holly berries before buzzing off again out of sight. This happens every year in this season.

Wren is picking his nesting sites again, along with his mate. They often try out several, making a number of false starts before settling to furnish one with eggs. Mr. Wren sings often and elaborately, often joined by his mate with complimenting phrases in duet.

Spring.

Reign of the Wren.

Wren out here, as one of my old friends would have said, "singing his ass off." And having a high old time of it in the process. Singing the same songs that have been sung here by the same bird for longer than a thousand years. Not the same individual, but even better, by sons of sons of sons of the original. Vigorous songs, complex and melodious.

Wren is joined presently by his wife, providing a simpler but complimentary counterpart to her husband's oration, making a duet for their own benefit, and for the benefit of listeners, as well. The message transmitted to all who hear—especially other wrens—couldn't be clearer: This territory is occupied by a hard-singing male, vigorous as a thunderstorm. Don't even think about setting foot on it. Be careful if you have to fly near the edge of it. And as for you unattached female wrens, you needn't think about moving in with this male singer, because, his duet partner clearly implies, you will hardly be welcomed by the resident female, herself as tough as a hard winter.

Their song keeps the territory safe for each of them. Ensures their exclusive rights to all wren resources located herein. And secures the future, when they will have responsibility for feeding and rearing the new family of youngsters that soon will hatch from their eggs, and be fledged to adulthood and supply wrens for the future of the country.

Life Resurgent.

An April morning bright and shiny as the Rocky Mountains in summer. Birdsong overflowing. Spring sweeping northward across the continent. New life in the meadows and woods. The flow of movement to icebound waters, resurgence of action in fishes, re-appearance of turtles and frogs, emergence of insects. And sweeping northward with the spring, a great movement of birds.

From the southern United States, from South America, Central America, and Mexico, a return to the country of their birth and a distribution of new life from the southern border of the United States to the Arctic Circle. More than fifty species of warblers to inhabit nearly every part of the northern continent; dozens of flycatchers; scarlet tanagers to the north and east, western tanagers to the mountain west; sandpipers, phalaropes, swans, and geese, pushing ever closer to breeding grounds at the northern extremes the continent.

> Sandy Creek was here,
> In forests of oak and beech,
> When flycatchers came.

The emergence of chipmunks, the birth of squirrels in the season of swelling buds and seed-pods, return of bats to patrol the evening skies; return of the gentle breeze, soft air, the bracing aroma of moisture, new grass, flowering blossoms. And soon underway, the maturing of new seeds, the birth of new generations of animals in advance of the fullness of summer.

> The stream slides smoothly
> Through flat-woods beneath the hills,
> Past dew-spangled leaves.

After the Storm.

Soon after the storm, the sky cleared in the west just in time to permit free passage of the rays of the setting sun. Bright light was concentrated beneath dark, scudding clouds that formed a low ceiling to the sky. The effect was arresting; the whole ordinary scene, illuminated by this light, shone in full substance, filled with objects representative of the cosmos and worthy of the mission—far more than magical.

Black Vultures.

Above the forest beside the river, three black vultures soared, masters of the wind. They slid along down the gravity line, losing altitude but gradually, making forty miles an hour without moving a feather. They made a wide turn into and around a thermal flow, invisible but for their use of it, and began spiraling upward, gaining altitude at fast pace, growing smaller and smaller to the sight, still hardly moving a wing, then resumed a course straight northward, again sliding swiftly across the high line of the landscape without noticeable alteration of posture, expending little effort beyond that needed to power their own nervous systems. Black vultures in the wind.

Birds near the River.

Cathy and I drove up to the Chickasaw Bluff north of Memphis and dropped off the ridge into the flood plain of the Mississippi River. Here were hundreds of acres of open crop land lined with sloughs and flooded swags beside the forested bluff and a mile away from the river. It is a good area for many kinds of wildlife, particularly waterfowl, raptors, and shorebirds.

The day was clear and sunny and the humidity was down. The visual clarity of the scenery was like that of a summer day in the West. Well out in an open field to the south we spotted several raptors sitting on the ground in the sunlight. There were two harriers (marsh hawks) and one red-tailed hawk. We stopped to look at these three and they flushed and flew away and two additional birds rose to the air from the near edge of the field, close upon a thick stand of grass at the field's border. They were short-eared owls! Rare birds for this area. Their distinctive shape and flight unmistakable. They were life birds for Cathy, and I had seen them myself only four or five times, the most recent being ten years ago.

There were still a few ducks hanging around the sloughs and flooded swags. Most of the shorebirds are still south of here, but we saw a couple of the tall and stately black-necked stilts, some of whom will nest here, and our common killdeer, an inland shorebird.

In an open field beside a forest of large bottomland hardwoods we found the first large group of swallows of the year. They were feeding on the wing above the open field. We walked out into the area until they were flitting just above our heads and right past our faces. There were three different species zipping around in one extended group: the large (for swallows) purple martins, rough-winged swallows, and the long-tailed, swallow-tailed barn swallows. (Most swallows have squared tails.) Swallows are so swift and maneuverable they seem to take little notice of people, just as hummingbirds don't.

At the edge of the forest we came across one of those little pockets of habitat that must have been perfect for the day and the particular conditions of the moment. It was, as we say, crawling with birds of more than a dozen species. We particularly enjoyed good looks at a golden-crowned kinglet and two fox sparrows. Neither species is uncommon but they are handsome and it is always nice to see them. They breed far to the north in Canada. We also found a winter wren, appropriately named for this area because we only find it in winter (or early spring). This was only the second we have found this year—our tiniest wren, one inch longer than a hummingbird.

Morning Below the Falls.

The young squirrel peaked out of her den in the early spread of light through the sky well before the sun reached the horizon. It was a cool morning in early spring and there was a mist of rain drifting through the leaves of the big woods. Her vision was keen as she searched the space about her, first moving only her eyes, then expanding her range by small and slow movements of her head. She was especially alert for movement but detected none beyond the slight sway of the leaves with the passage of the mist. She could hear the muted roar of the falls as the water of the creek above the cliff fell to plunge into the water and the creek-bed at her level of the mountain. The roar was a constant and a comfort in the world as she knew it. Anytime she moved up the creek and toward the falls, the roar got louder. She never went very near the falls because the roar was too loud there, and she depended on her hearing even more than her vision to alert her to the danger of predators. When she moved down the stream, the sound of the falls grew less, but she could still hear it for a long while.

A few months ago, after a major burst of courting behavior and some strangely interesting interactions with a dominant male squirrel, she had become dissatisfied with the leaf nest she had constructed last fall and had occupied through the winter. She was attracted to the more substantial nesting places afforded by holes and hollows in large trees, but many she found were already occupied by other squirrels who would not easily give them up and who did not encourage company. Then one morning after a stormy night of wind and rain she came across a place in a tree near her nest where the wind had ripped out a large branch near the trunk. The branch was hollow where it tore from the trunk, and there was a hollow area just inside the trunk where the branch had been attached. No one else had found nest hole before her and she was free to take possession, which she did immediately.

She went to work smoothing and enlarging her new den, easily gnawing away the wood until the hollowed area seemed to satisfy her as a fit home. She lined it with fresh leaves and grasses. On a night a couple of weeks ago she had given birth to four tiny and hairless pups and began nursing and caring for them full-time. It was the most riveting and satisfying activity she had ever experienced.

After a few minutes of looking and listening at the den's entrance, and finding nothing alarming in the reach of her senses, she emerged from her hollow and began to move down and around the tree, moving slowly and pausing often near the base of a large limb for more listening and looking before continuing her passage down the tree.

She crossed carefully and quietly through the tops of trees for a considerable distance until she arrived at an ash tree whose flower buds were a rich source of food at this time. She needed to eat well herself to assure good milk production for her babies.

Above the tops of the forest, unseen and undetected by the young squirrel, a mated pair of red-shouldered hawks worked through the air with acrobatic flight patterns. They were quite a distance apart but were keeping track of each other as well as watching intently for the movement of an animal in the forest below. They had fledglings back at the nest who hadn't been fed today.

At a certain moment, after both had been silent for a good while, one of the hawks broke out with a shrill hunting call, delivered at full volume. It repeated the call several times while its mate, its eyes searching as before for movement, remained utterly silent. The two often hunted in this way. The call of the screaming hawk might flush an animal into panicked movement below it, but it could also cause an animal in the distance to move toward a better hiding place. In that case, the silent partner might chance to see the movement and have an opportunity to attack.

The young squirrel was well up the height of the tree, still on the trunk and just below a large limb she was going to take out to its farther leaves when the jangling clarion of the hunting call of a hawk rang through the treetops. The sound was nerve shattering and made her want to run away at full speed. But a counter impulse warned her strongly against that action and, instead, she melted down against the bark of the tree trunk in a smooth flow of motion and became as still as any knot on the tree.

The frightening call was repeated again and again. The hawk seemed to be just above her hiding place. Yet the squirrel remained motionless. As still as a rock. She waited and waited. Then she heard the hunting call again, and the hawk had moved far away from her part of the forest. Still she waited. And she waited. She was nothing but patience, wanted nothing but to remain motionless. Many minutes after the hawks had left, she finally moved again, as though she gently shook off what had been an effective paralysis. Then she moved carefully out to where she could reach the succulent flower buds and began to eat.

She didn't hear the hawk calls any further. Maybe that hawk had made a kill already and stopped hunting for now. She fed long and well on the flower buds of the ash tree, then made her way back across the tree tops toward her den. After a while she began to hear the murmur of the falls in the distance, and as she continued on, the sound got gradually louder. It was still rather faint, though, when she arrived back at her den tree and went again to her pups. They snuggled up to her belly and began to nurse. There were four of them, and she was equipped with eight teats, so the pups had plenty to choose from. She lay on her side with her pups around her and it was warm and snug in the den.

Breeding Birds in the Big Woods.

Up in Shelby Forest, the big woods, the old forest at the height of spring, the peak of energy. Massive trees creating their own habitat, making their own unique environment—a place you feel at once is its own, where you are only a visitor, though welcome. You sense great power in the life that is rampant here—can't help but feel it, the stir of the breathing trees, the whisper of transactions with the least of breezes.

Today the forest is filled with birds and ringing with birdsong. The breeding migrants have joined the year-round residents. The year-rounders are well along with the season's procreation, maintaining their breeding territories, preserving their nests, eggs, and perhaps hatchlings, keeping up active relations with their mates. The new arrivals rush forward into the same tasks. Establish a territory, maybe the same one they had last year, find a mate, maybe last year's, if she has returned to the same territory again. Get on with the courtship and the nest-building. Get the brood started. Keep up your strength, get plenty to eat, and watch out for predators.

One new arrival is the indigo bunting, brilliant flash of shining aqua-blue at mid-height in the tops of bushes or the lower limbs of trees along the woods edges and the borders of fields. Its song is a long series of musical phrases, like those of some warblers, but contains several burry phrases and brusque stops to help you with the identification. The matchless wood thrush singing from the ground, or near it, in the midst of dense forest—a master of composition, each flute-like phrase sounding fresh as creation, even if it is one you have heard before. The parula warbler, handsome if you could catch a glimpse of it at the top of a tall deciduous tree, feeding among the highest leaves; it sings its buzzy, ascending trill every few seconds. The redstart, a real beauty of the forest, the male in bright orange and black, the female in softer colors of brownish-gray and yellow. She spreads her tail now and again to reveal its attractive yellow spots while the male repeats a short, musical song from mid-tree height.

The Kentucky warbler, a ground feeder, repeating its two-syllable, broken-note song between intervals of silence. The hooded warbler, among the brightest of the bright, but difficult to glimpse on its breeding grounds, staying low in the brush and dense plants well back in the forest; its bright, heavily inflected song is like a man's quick whistle. The prothonotary warbler, canary-bird, named for a yellow vestment of the Church, always near water, its song a series of clear, strong whistles, five or six in series and on nearly the same pitch.

Four of our flycatchers are here today, living up to their name, feeding on flying insects snatched from the air. One of them, the tiniest, is actually called a gnat-catcher. The pewee, a mid-sized flycatcher, is named for the sound of its beautiful and poignant call. You can see it actively surveying the skies from an open perch at mid-level. See it sally forth to catch its prey on the wing and then return again often to the same perch it just left. The so-called great-crested flycatcher, yet lacking much of a crest, but at least being rather great, or large, in size. It hunts the leaf tips at the upper story and the air above the treetops. "Wheep! Wheep!" it cries with vigor. The small Acadian flycatcher, half the size of a pewee, pint-sized and bull-headed, watching the air at low to mid-level; repeating its quick, sneeze-like call, often represented as "Peet-zah!" but sounding more, to me, like "Cheez-up!"

There are three caterpillar eaters among the group today. The white-eyed vireo, in low stuff around the edges of field and forest. Hard to see but easy to hear with it snappy, chipper song, a common phrase of which sounds to me like "Chip-to-the-rear, Chip-it!" The summer tanager, colored like a cardinal but without crest, and with a long, white bill that must be just right for dealing with big caterpillars. Frequent chipping calls of "Che-che-chew, che-che-che-chew!" drawing your attention to the treetop where he sits. And the large and powerful cuckoo (The common, yellow-billed variety; few people hereabout are so fortunate as to see the decidedly uncommon black-billed cuckoo.) looking as though it just arrived from the tropics. Locally known to many as the rain-crow, some people having taken his series of dawk-dawk-dawk calls, perhaps, as harbingers of rain.

Butterflies are everywhere in the forest today. The super-large yellow and black tiger swallowtail and the black and blue spicebush swallowtail; the medium-sized cloudless sulfur (yellow), the orange and black question mark (of deeply curved wings), the tastefully colored painted lady and the small, dusty blue spring azure. We came upon a big tiger swallowtail nourishing itself, as we thought, on residual moisture from a log beside the path. Then Cathy discovered what it was actually feeding on: The squashed carcass of a frog. Not exactly what she had wanted to see. "Gross!" she exclaimed. But good, I suppose, as far as the swallowtail was concerned.

Bird Work.

Down off the bluff and into the north Mississippi delta. Flat land, broad, long fields running to the big river, yellows and greens and browns in the sun, pale blue sky of wide open space. "Crops boiling out of the ground."

Many shorelines of sloughs and bayous and a few broad stands of trees left in the low spots within a wide-ranging land of row crops. Big cypress trees in natural lakes. Cathy and I are out here on the first of many trips to record breeding birds in this area, part of a statewide effort to compile a Mississippi breeding bird atlas. We are aiding the scientists of Mississippi State University as amateur ornithologists.

We begin with around thirty species for the first day. There won't be as many species on our territories in this agricultural terrain as in many study blocks of wider diversity. But the knowledge of who is breeding here is important to the construction of the atlas, the work is just as difficult and the care and skill needed to do it are the same here as anywhere else. It is a pleasure to be in the field enjoying the day and at the same time recording useful data on the bird life of the state.

Up early to get into the field soon enough to catch the birds at their vigorous morning songs and to have them singing for a good time after we arrive to hear them. That gives us a good chance to catch everything that is breeding in our area. Most species don't breed quietly but instead, do so with a great deal of singing. It is efficient to be able to record the presence of birds by their singing alone. Visual observation is important, too, but singing is part of breeding behavior, and that is what our survey is all about.

We found some beautiful bayou-and-lake habitat in our test blocks today, places with plenty of timber and some large cypress trees. The bird counts turned out higher. Totals of forty species in one block and forty-four in another; forty-nine different species, considering both blocks. The best find of the day for us were the least terns. They are a rare species for the interior of the state and unexpected in the agricultural land of the delta. They are nesting somewhere along the Mississippi River a few miles to the west. We saw at least sixteen of them, watching them dive headfirst into the water to catch fish.

Good butterflies in the yard at evening. Red admirals, painted ladies, the question mark. Cathy watered her flower beds near the side porch and saturated a portion of the lawn in doing so. The moisture brought up earthworms and the worms drew a husband-and-wife team of robins to work the wet area. They made a good harvest, capturing a couple of dozen worms with grace and apparent ease.

Mockingbird, Yard Boss.

This evening I went out to the camper to retrieve a beer from the refrigerator there, and found myself looking eye-to-eye with Mockingbird, perched in a tree a few feet above me. I undertook to provoke him by imitating the song of a towhee, one of the favorites that Mockingbird loves to mimic.

"Your tea, your tea. Drink your tea," I said. It was a decidedly poor imitation. I raised my voice to a falsetto to improve it and repeated the phrases again. Mockingbird immediately took up the same song, himself. "Your tea, your tea," he repeated five times in rapid succession. Mockingbird. Yard Boss.

Why so Beautiful?

I know science well and love it as well, I think, as a balanced person is likely to love it. And of all science, I admire the theory of evolution as one of the finest ideas of humankind. Yet when I contemplate evolution as a full account of human capability and experience, I return to that question. Why so beautiful? Perhaps I love this world so much because the development of that degree of love in my ancestors made them fight harder for life, fight harder to persevere, to find mates and to raise children. That is a good answer, but is it complete? The question remains: Why so beautiful? Why is it all so incredibly, heart-breakingly beautiful?

> Bright cedar branches
> Quickening to the motion
> Of feeding warblers.

Back in the Delta.

We have found two sets of juvenile birds in the past two days. Newly fledged killdeer chicks ran briskly all about between the two parents, who were about thirty feet apart. The chicks were half the size of the parents. I don't believe they can fly yet, but they surely can run. We also saw a strikingly marked juvenile bluebird—looking quite different from its parents. It was covered with triangular spots and looked something like an Aztec thrush.

I was touched by a tiny church we found well out in the farmland, in the rural countryside. Its name is Greater Peter's Rock. Clearly, it was built on almost no budget by people who had little money to spare for the project. It is only thirty by sixty feet in size, with a small lean-to room at the back, and is made of raw concrete blocks and unpainted wood paneling. It is roofed with shingles of three different colors in separate large patches. A few feet from the church-house on both sides are a small number of graves. Many of the graves—even the older ones—have no markers beyond the little metal placards provided by funeral homes. One grave has a simple wooden cross with the person's name carved into it by a knife. Several of the graves have good-quality, professionally made headstones. Two of these are inscribed "In loving memory," and one is inscribed "Beloved husband and father."

Bird Plumage: Who Can Afford Color?

Color, and the visual design of plumage, are among the most outstanding species characteristics of birds. As such, they make good focal points for a consideration of the evolution of species characteristics. There is tremendous variation in color, and in what we might call the *showiness* of plumage across the species.

A good deal of this variation can be understood as the striking of a balance between the competing influences of two basic propositions. Color enhances breeding success by contributing to territorial possession and mate attraction. Color threatens breeding success by increasing vulnerability to predation. We can envision color, then, as an expensive asset.

An explanation based on these competing influences works well in interpreting color variations observed in three of the most colorful groups of North American birds: The warblers, the tanagers, and the cardinals / grosbeaks. In the great majority of cases, males of these groups are more colorful than females. It is the male that must take possession of a breeding territory and attract a female mate to it. It is the female who must spend much more time at the nest incubating eggs and brooding hatchlings. Their more subdued coloration blends more readily into the background. Juveniles of these species also have this more protective coloration, sometimes more subdued even than that of adult females. Migratory males of nearly all species undergo a change in plumage at the close of the breeding season that decreases the showiness of their plumage, reducing their visibility during the non-breeding season.

If we look outside the three groups just considered to the broad range of North American birds, we encounter some interesting problems. What are we to think of the red-headed woodpecker? It is one of the most colorful species we know, yet the plumage is identical between males and females. We can explain this equality, perhaps, on the basis that mates of both genders defend their common territory and remain mates the year-round, perhaps for life.

We encounter a similar situation in the plumage of the familiar blue jay. The showy plumage is identical for the two genders. The advantage of outstanding plumage may involve the maintenance of social status in large winter feeding flocks. Identical plumage affords an equal opportunity for status in either gender. Young blue jays engage in extensive social interaction in courtship groups before mating for the first time. After that, they may recognize a former mate as an individual throughout the year and choose the same mate again at the next breeding season.

Thus, where we find colorful plumage we can usually suggest compelling contributions that may have led to the evolutionary selection of this expensive characteristic. Why colorful plumage should have evolved in some species but not in others is a harder question to address. The answers must rest on detailed information about the particular situation faced by each species. Many species, such as most wrens, thrushes, vireos, and titmice possess subdued plumage year-round and also lack plumage distinctions between males and females. The relative distinction of one male to another in these species must be a matter of gender-specific behavior characteristics.

Evolution operates over great expanses of time. Over the vast stretch of time, many variations in individual characteristics occur. Natural selection through survival and successful reproduction merely chooses the most successful of these variations. The environment is composed of a wide variety of habitats, and a wide array of possible strategies may succeed within that complex.

Summer.

The Charge of a Cat.
Late in the afternoon Cathy and I watched from the side porch as a neighborhood cat began making a stalk from beneath one of our cars toward the flower bed twenty-five yards away. Following the line of the cat's focus, we saw a chipmunk making its way down the length of the bed. As the chipmunk passed behind a tree trunk, preventing visual contact between the two animals, the cat began an all-out charge at a spot just past the tree where the chipmunk must re-appear. In a close escape, the chipmunk made it into a clump of thick brush. The chipmunk was safe. But inexplicably it emerged at the far end of the clump and the cat charged explosively and caught the chipmunk, quickly maneuvering its body to achieve a bite to the nape of its neck. And just that quickly the career of the chipmunk was ended. Perhaps it was young and inexperienced. It was too nervous to remain in its safe hiding place, and it froze for just too long as the cat charged. The cat had won a great victory, but the chipmunk's loss was even greater. As

Carlos Castaneda might have said, its time to roam this marvelous world was over.

Canoeing at Spring Lake.

In the clear spring water of the lake we saw two tightly packed schools of fingerling bass only a few days removed from the nest of their birth. We slipped close to large carps many times, getting so close that they sprinted away through the shallows throwing up large humps of water in their wakes.

After taking a good look around we settled into a fishing mode. I maneuvered the canoe while Cathy fished with her spinning outfit, working a plastic worm along the bottom near the cypress trees of the lake. She tried worms of several colors and used different types of retrieves but caught nothing. She threw some good casts into places where they must have been. She is a patient fisher. She claimed to have a good bite two or three times but produced no fish. If you know Cathy, you'll know she must have asked several times if I wouldn't like to take over the fishing and let her handle the canoe, but I preferred handling the boat. When both of us can't fish at once, I'd rather watch her fishing than to fish, myself.

A Regal Retrieve.

In the afternoon we fished at a pond out at brother David's house. Cathy hung a good-sized bass and was bringing it in when Regal, a big, friendly, overweight yellow Labrador with arthritis plunged into the water and took out swimming to get Cathy's fish. Cathy did alright as long as she could keep the fish underwater, but as she got it in close to the bank it came up to the surface. Regal made a lunge and caught the fish in his jaws, swam away from Cathy up to the bank, and took off for the house with the fish in his mouth. My brother made a grab at the line and pulled, but it was no match for the eighty-five pound Regal and immediately snapped. David had to chase him nearly a quarter-mile to get the fish back. Regal's arthritis didn't seem to bother him when he was running away with the fish.

A Dove's Last Flight.

Cathy and I were walking along the edge of a parkland field in Dead Horse Ranch Park, Arizona. The field extended on a level plain to the north bank of a river a quarter mile away. Above the edge of the field was a rocky ridge eighty feet high grown sparsely in desert shrubs. A dove flew out from the base of the ridge and a hawk rose from a point halfway up the ridge and flew in pursuit of the dove.

It was a Cooper's hawk and probably a female as judged by its size. The dove immediately went into maximum speed flying, but the hawk closed in nevertheless. The dove veered in its direction several times and the hawk bored in on it, matching it turn for turn like a sidewinder missile. The dove made it halfway to the river before it was caught by the hawk in midair and carried to the ground in a scatter of loosed feathers.

Early Summer.

I wish I could write the light of an early night in June. Long extended twilight with the first lightning bugs of the season sprinkling the dark with light and the first bats of the summer flitting about just beneath the tree branches catching their supper meals. In those early days, we often had Chuck-Will's-widows singing at night right there in town.

Sometimes after dusk, we would play kick-the-can around the tall, wide two-story house on the slight ridge above the roadway. Friends would walk over from up the street and across town. All of the game's pursued could more or less stay together, or at least could know where the others were hiding. If they wished, a group of them could stand together behind the house with guards watching the approach from each side so they would know when the pursuer, the one who was It, was coming. By contrast, the *It* person had a lonely job, he was against the rest of the group in total. He had to tag them and take them back to home base (the can) one at a time. They were duty bound to wait there until someone who hadn't been tagged yet could sneak past the It, beat him back to home base, and kick the can before the It could reach the can and count the charger out. Often much time was required before all the hiders were caught and assembled in one group at the can. When that was finally accomplished, a new It could be chosen and a new game begin.

We would play until we were worn out. Then our friends would go back to their own homes, and we would go upstairs to the bedroom over the street and lie on the cool sheets and wait for the good breeze of the oscillating fan to pass over us again as it made its rounds of the room all through the night. Always, long before morning, we would reach for the sheet and pull it over us for cover.

Some mornings I would wake at first light, and get dressed and down the stairs early enough to go with Goldie across the street and through the pasture up to the barn to milk the cows at dawn. I wasn't any account as a milker and didn't do much of it, although Goldie instructed me in the procedure several times. Instead, I would watch him and the cows and enjoy the rich smells of the barn. I would climb up into the loft and smell the fresh hay in the heavy morning air.

You could get out from the loft onto an extending porch roof at the back of the barn above the yard where the cows waited until Goldie would let them in to be milked. Once when I was out on the roof looking down on a collection of cows, I got the idea it would be a good joke to make a run at them from atop the roof and holler and wave my arms when I got to the edge and scare all the cows. Without further thought, I started running down the sloping tin roof toward the cows. But as I neared the edge and tried to stop, I went sliding out of control on the dew-slick surface of the roof, and before I even got off a yell, went careening down among the cows, barely missing two cow's backs and hitting hard on my feet and turning my ankle. It didn't scare the cows at all.

Since I hadn't managed to get off a yell, it turned out that Goldie, inside the barn, hadn't noticed what I had done, and I was able to hobble into another section of the barn before he saw me. About that time it occurred to me that if I had succeeded in hollering and scaring the cows, Goldie would have been certain to take notice and make an appropriate comment about how long it might take me to learn to have better sense. But he never suspected anything as far as I know. I sat around nursing my ankle for a while and then walked back to the house beside Goldie, hobbling as little as I could manage.

Later I told Daddy I had made a jump I shouldn't have tried and hurt my ankle. He examined it and told me it wasn't sprained but was just badly strained. He wrapped it with an elastic bandage and told me to keep my weight off of it as much as I could and rest it for a couple of days. He was right, and after a day or two the ankle didn't bother me anymore. I never said much for a long time about my fool's run down the roof of the barn to land among the cows.

Still Spring.

June 7: According to my schedule, summer (June through August) is fully underway, yet the air this morning is fresh and bracing as the Rocky Mountains, lively and cool as Mississippi in mid-October. Breathe with full appreciation. Feel it touch against your skin. The experience is deeply satisfying, like sitting down to a fine meal. This morning it is still spring. We get days like this often until very near the end of official spring on June 21.

Thunder Storm.

A big storm came across the River and tore into the west side of DeSoto County at mid-morning. I was over there at the time looking for birds. A huge, high cloud bank menaced across the River, building higher and darker, plenty of electricity shooting straight to the ground in bright bolts and staying bright for a moment in prolonged release of voltage; strong, gusting winds blowing hundreds of leaves from trees as in a foretaste of autumn. Barn swallows whipped around the sky like fighter planes, glorying in the massive and changing air flow. Then rain in quick, small-duration bursts from the edge of the dark wall; then a flooding downpour.

The tremendous down-flow of air from the top of the cloud wall at the passage of the storm dropped the temperature from the nineties straight into the low seventies. The overcast that lasted through the afternoon kept the day cool right through to twilight.

Late June.

The volume of birdsong is down now after the Solstice. The early mornings are soft and warm, rather quiet, with the singing, perhaps, of a single cardinal and the drone of one or two cicadas. New baby birds continue to appear foraging with their parents about the trees and lawns. They have been abundant for more than a month and will be seen throughout the remainder of the summer. They stand out from the adults in their immature plumage, in some instances, but more in the lack of finesse and expertise in their movements and actions. Many don't seem to respect grave dangers in their new environments, such as the near approach of a dog or a person. Their attempts at foraging appear half-hearted and inept. Many are still fed largely by their parents. But the parents have brought the young ones into the foraging environment with them, where the young can observe the parents' movements and can have a chance to take advantage themselves of any opportunities that appear before them.

Two very young chimney swifts fell into our den fireplace last night. Our dog, Pilot, sensed them immediately. I took Pilot outside while Cathy retrieved the baby swifts and took them outside and let them attach with their claws to the bricks at the side of the house. She said they were moving their wings around as though they might be ready to fly very soon. This morning she checked the wall of the house where she had left them and both were gone and were not on the ground below, either, so we are free to think they matured enough during the night to fly off on their own with still a possibility, maybe a decent one, of surviving.

Last Cool Morning.

Today was one of the last cool mornings we can expect to have before late August or maybe September. It is June 26. After the hot as July weather we have had for the past few days, the day felt more like early fall than late spring.

Cathy and I went out to the Park early to walk a couple of miles before the day warmed up fully. The geese and ducks have multiplied hugely there over the past few weeks. The babies are almost adult-sized but are still walking around under the protection of their parents. Many of them will not survive their first year, but enough will survive to supply a steady increase in the numbers of waterfowl inhabiting the two lakes of the park. There already are far more birds on the lakes than the terrain can support without damage. Yet they increase every year despite the work of the coyotes. Local golf courses, with their own lakes, have a similar problem.

Coldwater.

When I was growing up and my father or my Uncle Mack said something about the River, or sometimes they would call it the Creek, I knew they were talking about our favorite stream in the world, the Coldwater River. It was a favorite swimming hole about five miles from our home and we went there to swim on many a hot afternoon. We boys would swim in the broad bend of the river and take turns running off the high bank at the end of a rope swing and dropping into the water well out in the stream. There was a gravel bar just downstream of the swimming hole where the entire flow of the river was compressed into a narrow stream only three feet deep, and the flow of the current was swift and strong, and we loved to play in it and beside it.

Our father and Uncle Mack would swim up the river the entire length of the bend well past where we boys would go, swim back to the lower end of the hole, and stand waist deep in the river for a few minutes.

Then Daddy would spend an hour or more fishing in the river nearby while Uncle Mack would watch us boys playing in the current of the narrows. Occasionally he would walk upriver and check with Daddy about how the fish were biting.

Now, the Coldwater really is a cold river. We always heard it is so because it receives a heavy flow from cold springs. But I never knew what the proof of the cold springs was, other than the coldness of the river. Hitting the water even on the hottest of days literally took your breath away, and it seemed impossible that you would be able to tolerate staying in it for any length of time. But then, almost miraculously you would *get used to it* again, as in past swimming trips, and the cold water would become merely bracing and refreshing rather than freezing.

One week during a really hot spell of summer, back in the days before anyone had air conditioning, word got around town that Morgan Loftin, finding it too hot to sleep, got his wife up, called his children from bed—all buddies and cousins of mine—loaded the family into his car, and drove to the swimming hole. He got an old tire and burned it on the bank for a light, and the family enjoyed a cold and refreshing swim before heading back home to bed, their skins still cool from the river. Folks found the story amusing, but the main feeling they had about it was admiration for Morgan's bold action.

Ponds We Fished In.

Norvel's Lake was owned by Joe Norvel, a son of one of the oldest merchant families in Olive Branch. He still ran one side of the old store, offering mostly dry goods and a little hardware by the time I was reaching high school, and he tended the store all day every day except Sunday. He rented out the other side of the store. It was devoted to groceries, and I worked there for a couple of years sacking and checking out. In the mornings Mr. Norvel mostly read the Memphis paper and worked the crossword puzzle. I don't remember noticing what he did in the afternoons, maybe read a magazine or a novel. He needed something to occupy himself with between the infrequent visits of customers to his store.

Joe Norvel lived in a fine, near mansion-sized old house rendered in the English Tudor style just to the north edge of the commercial area of town. The house sat well back off the road atop a low knoll of good lawn and flower gardens. A quarter mile down the slope from the house, in an idyllic parkland of meadow and old trees, at the center of a shallow valley, stood the lake. It was maybe four and a half acres in size, with many trees standing just at its edges. It was surrounded by meadows in which only a few milk cows ever grazed, and its waters were always clear, even after a big rain. The waters were clear, but they had a black look as you stood on their banks. So we thought of it as a blackwater lake—a purely clear lake. You couldn't find a prettier or more inviting place to be on a nice day in spring or early summer.

Mr. Norvel didn't mind if people came on the

property and fished in the lake, and they came from all over town. They just crossed the barbed wire fence and walked right in. No one needed to bother asking permission. I was at the lake hundreds of times during my childhood, with my brothers and my father, with my friends, and often, by myself. I think I can recall seeing Mr. Norvel at the lake only one time over all those years, and that time I think he must have recognized my father's car parked on the road near the lake.

Anyway, as I recall, he walked down across the pasture from his house and came up and greeted Daddy in a friendly manner, and they talked for a good while before Mr. Norvel walked back home. He and Daddy had grown up together and were friends, even though Mr. Norvel's family had some claim, or maybe just a pretension, to aristocracy, and had sent their son to a fancy boy's school and to Sewanee University. Both Daddy's and Mr. Norvel's fathers had been merchants in town when they grew up, and their stores faced each other across the town 'square.'

It was always said there were some really big bass in Norvel's Lake, and I remember the story that someone had caught a nine pound bass there a couple of years before. The lake was easy to fish. There were many shady places all around its edge and plenty of wide openings between the trees so that you could walk around the bank and cast a bass plug to reach almost any place you wanted to fish. Except the middle part of the lake, of course. No one could cast anywhere nearly that far. So, naturally, we boys thought that if we just had a boat and could get out to the middle we would be sure to catch a lot of fish.

Eventually I learned on my own that you can usually catch lots more fish around the edges than at the middle of a lake, but the middle was what we couldn't get at and so that is where we wished we could fish. Anyway, no one had a boat and we all fished around the edges. It was pretty unusual for any of us to catch a bass in Norvel's Lake, and I never saw anyone catch one larger than a pound-and-a-half or two pounds in size. But we always thought someone would catch another big one there, and the lake and the clear water and the scenic setting were so attractive that we always enjoyed fishing there, fished with high hope, and loved being there.

Now what was true with respect to the bass in Norvel's Lake was the opposite of what was true for the bream there. The lake had large, brilliantly colored bream in it, and you could catch them with regularity. They were as big as bream get in our part of the country, and a full-sized one was a good deal broader and a little longer than a man's hand, and was more than an inch thick. They could pull at a ratio of three or four times what you would expect for their size and, buddy, was it a lot of fun to catch one. You could catch them on crickets or worms with a cane pole, but you could catch even more, and have a lot more fun doing it, with a fly rod.

There was a long neck of the lake at the upper end on the east side where I loved to fish with a fly rod. The part of the neck I liked to fish was sixty or seventy yards long, so it was possible for a couple of us boys to fish it with fly rods at the same time. That way we could see what each of us was catching—on a slow day, it was fun to see your buddy catch a fish even if you couldn't catch one—and we could have a competition and see who could catch the most. We would keep a close count on the number we caught. Usually we would just bring them in, take a good look at them, add them to our count, of course, and then release them back into the lake. Even though we were releasing them, we hated it when one dropped off our hook just after we pulled the fish from the water. We hadn't caught it, then, we had only almost caught it. We didn't get to take a good look at it, and worst of all, we couldn't count it.

If you were standing almost anywhere along the east side of the neck where I preferred to fish, there was plenty of open space behind you for a good back cast and you could throw anywhere you liked out toward the center of the neck. Toward the upper end of the neck, pretty much the upper third of it, you could cast, with a good, long throw, from the bank where you stood all the way across the neck to the trunks of the cypress trees and willows lining the opposite bank. It took a good cast to do it, but if you could lay your fly softly well in under the low branches up near the base of a cypress tree on the other bank, you would usually be rewarded by an immediate strike, and would have the fun of wrestling a big bream all the way across the width of the neck to bring it in to the lake's edge at your feet.

That was the most demanding use of a fly rod that I ever found, growing up, and it was the most fun and the most honest in its payoff. When you threw a perfect cast in there, you had a good chance of getting a fish every time. It gave you the feeling of being an artist to fish like that. A mediocre cast might pay off sometimes, but a perfect cast had a much greater chance. And even if it didn't pay off, you had the satisfaction of having placed it with perfection—of seeing it land in that perfect placement with the softness of a bug dropping gently to the water's surface. I always counted it a good afternoon when I could catch a dozen of those big, beautifully colored bream at Norvel's Lake. Often I caught fifteen or twenty of them. But whether you caught them or not, you always were glad to have spent time in a place like that practicing a skill that you loved. Leaving the lake, it was as though you had been to a fine restaurant and enjoyed the pleasure of eating an excellent meal.

Gene's Lake was owned by Gene Alexander, a neighbor of ours and a good friend of my father's and my Uncle Mack's. He put in the lake to have a permanent source of water for his beef cows. The lake stood not over a quarter-mile from the back door of our house across a cow pasture, over a low hill, and in a shallow draw on the other side. We always just went out the back door, over the wire fence, and walked to the lake. It was formed by damming the flow of a small stream and made a body of water maybe three and a half acres in a shape that was about three times as long as it was wide up the length of the draw.

The lake lay near the center of an eighty acre piece of land that had once belonged to our family, on the McNeill—my grandmother's—side. Her brother Harvey McNeill had owned it and lived there while he was a doctor in the town. But he died in his mid-forties and the land passed on to his widow who, in time, married Gene Alexander. Then after many years, she died before he did, and the land passed on to him. Much later, when Gene himself died, he left his estate to a young man of no relation to him who had built a house next door to Gene's and whose family had been kind to the aging Gene for a number of years. So that is how the land on which Gene's Lake stood passed out of our family. But during the time I was growing up, Gene was still alive, was good friends with our family, and was glad to have us fish in his lake.

I fished at the lake at sun-up, sun-down, and at all hours of the day in between. I fished there with my brothers and my father and my friends and by myself. I caught many hundreds of bass there, some big ones, too, and had my line broken by some that were as big as I couldn't help but imagine them to be, once they were lost and I would never be able to see just how big they were. I remember catching a bass over four pounds in size on a fly rod and a bream fly one Sunday afternoon when I was at the lake alone. I gave that fish to a black woman who was a friend of mine and told her to be sure and mention how big it was to one of my friends and fishing competitors who lived nearby.

It was easy to fish Gene's Lake because there were not many trees around it and you could walk all around its circumference easily. Its depth increased gradually as you waded toward the center from anywhere except next to the levee of the dam, and I learned to wade out as I pleased and thus greatly increased the surface area of the water that was open to my fishing. Gene's Lake was never as clear as Norvel's Lake, but it was nearly always semi-clear and good to fish in. It had a good enough flow of water into it that it stayed pretty much the same size all the time.

Often after a big rain my brothers and my friends and I would go over to the lake and catch small fish that were being swept from the lake in the large flow of water from the spillway. There were dozens and dozens of baby bream and bass in the flow, and we caught them in buckets and in homemade seines and sometimes by watching for one to drift past and shoveling it out onto the bank with our hands. We kept our prizes in other buckets and had them for use as bait if we wished. More likely we would just look at them for a while then, having possessed them to our satisfaction, and retaining our pride in having caught so many of them, we would simply return them to the lake. I remember other times when we carried them overland to other lakes and ponds and released them there, and I feel sure I went back to some of those other places we had stocked and caught again some of the fish we had put in there years before, ourselves.

Gene's Lake was a great boon to my boyhood. We went swimming in it on hot afternoons, skinny-dipping. We made forts in the folds of land around the lake and lobbed dirt clods back and forth between the forts. And the lake was good for the use of a fly rod against bream. The water being less clear than that of Norvel's Lake, and the lake itself not nearly as old, its bream were not nearly as deeply colored and not quite as large as those from Norvel's. But they bit good. I remember an afternoon in early spring when I stood almost in one place and caught bream after bream, hooking one almost every cast, until I had caught more than seventy.

Roxie was a large—though not tall—black woman who cooked for my grandmother, and then for my family after Grandmother died, and who had a good part in raising me. I say she was a black woman, but her complexion really was nowhere near black but was of a lighter shade than milk chocolate. As a child, I thought of her as being old, but she was a vigorous woman and probably still in her mid-fifties at the time. She was Goldie's wife, and they lived in their own small house a short distance from the back door and kitchen of our house. They always ate breakfast in our kitchen and often ate their other meals there, as well. They nearly always just ate what we ate—what Roxie had fixed for all of us.

Roxie loved to fish, and she often took me with her across the street and up a lane to fish at pond we called Drew's Lake because it was owned by a man named Drew Birmingham. Gene's Lake had not been built by this time. Roxie had her own advice on fishing summed up in a verse she had memorized. I've heard some of this from other sources but never heard all of it except from Roxie:

Wind from the West, the fish bite best;
Wind from the East, the fish bite least;
Wind from the South blows the bait in their
    mouth;
Wind from the North, they turn their tail and
    snort.

I still dream about the old Gravel Pit. In the dream, I am always walking or maybe driving in a car around the streets of the old Olive Branch of my boyhood when I'm struck with the recollection of a small mountain range near the town that I had forgotten about for a time. I go to investigate and find myself winding uphill on a twisting gravel road and coming at last to a rugged mountain basin, with peaks rising in front of me and a mountain ridge standing on my right side. That basin of my dream represents the reality of the most exotic, in many ways the most scenic, and certainly the most unusual place we visited, fished, and camped in our boyhood around Olive Branch, the Gravel Pit. It was what remained of an extensive gravel quarry, long since filled with water in its low areas, where the mining operations had ceased four decades before.

The lane from the main road to the Gravel Pit led gently uphill, yet as you came over a slight rise and down to an extensive flat expanse of sand and rock at the edge of the water, there rose on the other side of the lake almost shear gravel cliffs up to eighty feet higher than the basin. The lake itself was shaped roughly like a horseshoe, but one in which the two prongs of the horseshoe were five or six times wider than the connecting arc at the top. The horseshoe was laid out with the open end toward the spot where the lane from the road led to the edge of the lake. It was like two different lakes, one falling off steeply from its banks on three sides and very deep, and one falling off only gradually from its banks and more shallow in maximum depth. The lane into the lake ended at the inside edge of the deep-water side of the horseshoe and five acres of flat sandy soil separated that spot from the inner edge of the other side of the horseshoe on the shallow side of the lake. The deeper side of the lake was about eight acres in size and the shallower side was about four acres.

The deep side of the lake was very rocky and gravelly around most of its circumference, with steep, high banks on its left, or north side. On its inner south side, on the half nearer the connecting arc of the horseshoe, the bank was low and covered with a thick growth of willows, and the water-depth increased gradually, and you could wade out quite a ways to fish that side, as you could do, as well, on much of the shallower side of the double lake.

There was a race of large, colorful lizards that inhabited the sandy land between the two branches of the lake. They were six-lined racers seven inches long and as quick as thought. We always loved to see those lizards, and we didn't know any other place anywhere around the town that you could find them. The rocky, sandy soil—with many expanses of almost pure gravel lying on he surface—was a fine source of fossils. Sometime during my year in the seventh grade, my science teacher, Mrs. Merrill, taught us about the crinoids and corals that used to live in the inland sea that covered this area of the Earth hundreds of thousands of years ago. She told us you could still find lots of fossils of these creatures in the native gravel hereabouts, as well as the gravel of many roads and driveways in the area, because nobody hauled gravel any farther than he had to, and so any of the gravel we encountered was likely to be native gravel from someplace nearby.

I became fascinated with finding crinoid fossils and

searched for them and found them in plenty all around town. The Gravel Pit was my all-time favorite place to look for them, both because there was an unlimited supply of new gravel to inspect there, and it was fossil-rich, but also I could be surrounded by the exotic scenery and environment there while searching.

There was always good bass fishing at the Gravel Pit and always the chance of catching a really big one. My father caught a four-and-a-half-pounder there early along in our experience of fishing the place. I believe it was the largest bass he ever caught, although he caught quite a few other big ones. Later, he turned almost entirely to catching catfish out of the Coldwater River on trot lines and caught many catfish much larger than his largest bass. He was very successful with the catfish and kept it up vigorously until he passed away. At the time, I remember someone down town saying, sadly, "Well, I guess there'll be more catfish in the Coldwater River after this."

Several of my fishing buddies also caught big bass at the Gravel Pit, but I never caught a four-pounder there. I caught a lot of nice ones and several that would have gone three pounds. But the largest bass I ever hooked there—or maybe anywhere—broke my line right at the bank when I couldn't help but to try my hardest to haul him out when I saw how big he was. But he was stronger than I was and actually managed to pull my straining forearms back toward the water. I could see him clearly almost out of the water and right against the bank. Then the line broke and he was gone. I always thought he would have weighed seven and a half pounds, but then they always get bigger when you know you've lost them and will never see them again, especially if they've broken your line.

The fish may not have been as huge as I thought, but that is what I thought, anyway. Maybe you can guess how heartsick I was at his loss. If only I hadn't strained against the line so hard...but I couldn't help myself. It was a full three minutes later that the floating lure I had been using rose to the surface where I was able to retrieve it. It had taken the big fish that long to shake the hook from its mouth. If only I could have been a little calmer and a little more patient, almost surely I would have caught it. The biggest bass ever to come out the Gravel Pit. Maybe even a ten pounder. But instead, I had broken the line.

The Fate of a Swallow

A brilliant summer morning still fresh with spring. The dew still bright on the grass and the countryside shining like an Impressionist landscape. The scene suggestive of a soundtrack by Beethoven: the Sixth Symphony, Pastorale.

At the bottom of a hill, a clear stream crossed the road and ran out into a large, open pasture covering the floor of a valley, I stopped the car and got out. I walked across the bridge over the stream toward a spot where a group of barn swallows flew back and forth, feeding on the wing. As I reached the far end of the bridge, two or three swallows flew up from the roadbed where they had been sitting. Another was sitting there that didn't fly up. It couldn't fly. One of its wings had been badly broken. It must have had other severe injuries, too, because it was unable even to crawl away. Perhaps it had flown into a car earlier in the morning. It occurred to me that the other birds I had seen sitting with it may have been its parents or siblings. It was obviously a young bird not long out of the nest.

Then I noticed the ants had already found it. A number of them crawled over its feathers and a thin column of them traded to and fro in a line that led to the injured bird. I thought it was too bad the bird's accident hadn't killed it outright, or that some other car coming by later hadn't chanced to kill it already. But there was little traffic out here. The bird might remain alive there with the ants, on the roadbed in the increasing heat of the sun, for several hours yet. I turned and walked back to the car, pulled it up and positioned it carefully, and ran over the injured bird, crushing it flat beneath a tire. I got out and looked again, to make sure the job had been cleanly done, then drove on. But as I drove, I began to question whether I had done the right thing in dispatching the injured bird. To be sure, I had done so in sympathy with its plight and for the sole reason of ending its suffering in a hopeless cause. Yet who was I to say when a bird should die, or what experiences it should be denied?

Events like this one are deeply disturbing. Yet they happen at every moment, to people as well as to birds and other creatures. What are we to think of them?

A few years ago there was a popular song with the title: *If I Ruled The World*. Tony Bennett sang it. If you recall the lyrics of that song, which formed a good match with its melody, they were strongly sentimental, overly sweet, cloying almost to the point of revulsion.

These characteristics didn't appear to hurt the song's popularity. On the contrary, it was quite successful and must have pleased many people. Everything in the world of this song was just hunky-dory, just grand, and all guaranteed.

But is that the sort of world we really want? One where everything always works out perfectly as in the formula of a sappy Disney movie? Or can we conceive a better world, one that commands meaningful commitment, one that rivets attention?

What about a world, not where anything goes, but where anything physically possible does go? A world that conforms to probabilities but constantly deals up a share of surprises, too? Where anything that can happen will happen, does happen, to someone? A world that gives members of our human species—with superbly developed brains and ability to judge circumstance and consequence—the chance to control things to an important degree by the choices we make and the care and skill with which we act? That gives us at least a degree of spontaneous and free reign to make our own way among always surprising and exciting possibilities? I propose a world where the stakes are high, where we can go either right or wrong, succeed or fail, a world with compelling occasions for both joy and despair.

This is to be a world of immense meaning, where every action has consequences for all the future. The story is not preordained, not already "in the book," but rather is created by ourselves as we go, and by all elements of the vast skein of life, in the details of their individual lives. Yes, this is a world worthy of literature, worthy of LIFE. Let us have it at once! And have it we can. All we need do is realize it is the very world that surrounds us at this moment. For my part, I do not care to imagine a better one.

Leibniz wrote: "...the more we are enlightened and informed in regard to the works of God the more will we be disposed to find them excellent and conforming entirely to that which we desire."

Even so, there remains the problem of our own mortality. It's easy to be discomfited by the thought that, at the end of our struggles and adventures, we may simply become nothing. If we stop to examine it seriously for a moment, however, the idea of simple immortality may not seem so great, either.

The actual circumstance of immortality–like the assurance of happiness and success–would rob life of much of its meaning. Suppose we were to find that after years of struggle we had finally managed to accomplish the very thing we had worked for for so long. What difference would it make? After all, we had forever to obtain the accomplishment. What difference if we fail at this or that particular chance, in this or that particular year or decade? No difference–we have forever at our disposal. What if we botch this particular marriage? No matter, we can have an infinity of marriages. The same with children. The same with beautiful days, shining mountains, sparkling streams. Is one more splendid than another? Why bother with this particular mountain, this particular man or woman, this very day and moment? Who cares? After all, "There's a million of 'em."

The overwhelming and riveting fact is that our individual lives do come to an end. Yet the system that fostered them continues. In several ways, at least, we continue with it. The ongoing world will bear the imprint of our actions far beyond the end of our lives. And the molecules of our bodies won't be going anywhere. They continue here in the system; they can't possibly escape it. And perhaps there is more. We can't say exactly what. We are well aware of religious teachings on the afterlife. Still, perhaps no one can imagine, with the conviction of physical reality, just what a non-physiological existence will be like. Even Jesus is recorded as having asked that the cup of death be passed from him. What else may we say on the subject?

The American writer Edward Abbey was a hard-nosed realist, a tightly focused proponent of the physical. Time and again in his work he expressed a fierce disdain of the overly sentimental, the "pie-in-the-sky" conception of the world and our place in it. Yet years after publishing the book *The Brave Cowboy*, he came to believe he had made a mistake in ending it with a frank description of the death of Jack Burns, the protagonist. He didn't regret describing the physical destruction that was Burns's fate but said he wished he had finished with a scene in which Burns's body could not be found but had mysteriously disappeared, so that no one could ever be sure just what had become of it.

Baruch Spinoza—accepted by many as the greatest philosopher of the modern era—included the following among the closing remarks of his greatest work: " . . . the wise man, in so far as he is considered as such, is scarcely ever moved in his mind, but being conscious by a certain eternal necessity of himself, of God, and of things, never ceases to be, and always enjoys true peace of soul."

The teachings of the Chinese philosopher Laotse expressed the foundation of the Taoist religion and were central to the development of the Zen branch of Buddhism. It is notable in itself that Laotse made few statements directly addressing the question of mortality. His view is implicit in the following verse:

> It has been said that he who is a good preserver of
>   his life
> Meets no tigers or wild buffaloes on land,
> Is not vulnerable to weapons on the field of battle.
> The horns of the wild buffalo are powerless
>   against him;
> The paws of the tiger are useless against him;
> The weapons of the soldier cannot avail
>   against him.
> How is it so?
> Because he is beyond death.

Here are the thoughts of three poets/philosophers of America.

Emerson:
We live in succession, in division, in parts, in particles. Meantime within man is the soul of the whole; the wise silence; the universal beauty, to which every part and particle is equally related; the eternal ONE. And this deep power in which we exist, and whose beatitude is all accessible to us, is not only self-sufficing

in every hour, but the act of seeing, and the thing seen, the seer and the spectacle, the subject and the object, are one.

One sees that Emerson's view provides not only for the philosopher but for the injured barn swallow, as well.

Whitman:
All goes onward and outward, nothing collapses,
And to die is different from what anyone supposed, and luckier.

And Thoreau:
One world at a time!

Old Oaks of Town.

Many of the huge oaks we, as boys, used to walk beneath and play among still stand in the town today. It is a privilege to pass among them. I take pleasure in them now, as I did as a boy. They are hundreds if not thousands of years old—five or six feet thick, eighty or more feet tall. We used to enjoy thinking how the Chickasaws had hunted and camped beneath them before there was a State of Mississippi and a town of Olive Branch.

The trees look the same now as they did when I was a boy. I remember my father, well along in his life, saying they looked the same as when he and my uncle Mack were boys. Maybe they will look the same in another hundred years and beyond. Long and long may they shine.

First Cicadas.

The first cicadas of the year, locusts, what my father called July flies, sang this morning for the first time this year—and, of course, for the first time ever in their lives. There were only a few, but they began to chorus to a degree from the outset. They have made their way out of the ground where they lived as grubs and crawled out onto the surface as pupae and shed their skins and sprouted their wings and became adults. They will live for quite a few weeks—many will still be here singing in mid-August. They will find mates with their singing, make fertilized eggs, lay them in the earth, and then the cycle of their lifespan will be finished and they will simply run out of vital energy and die, sometimes coming into pieces as they reach the end. I recall a time that one of them flew to a landing on my brother Hugh's shoulder, had both its wings snap off and helicopter to the ground, then fell dead, simply sliding off Hugh's shoulder and bouncing on the ground to lie still.

The date of their appearance above ground this year is a little early if judged by my father's appellation of them as July flies, but we are but a day or two from the summer solstice and so almost into July. I look forward to many of their choruses over the coming weeks, when it will seem as though dozens are singing in unison or in alternating cadence with each other. But I know one of these large and robust bugs can make plenty of noise by itself. So I expect eight or ten of them could sound like a good many more than that.

Inevitably I will tire of hearing them before they are gone again for a year. Then, upon noting their profound silence for a few days, I will think of them with fondness and will miss them a little. The homey sound of their music stirs good memories.

His Last Song of Summer?

Mockingbird has stopped singing! Has had nothing to say for three days, now. He continues to patrol his realm, but seems to have assumed his winter role in patrolling it. He has chased several birds from his area but has been utterly silent. For the first time in five months. Five months of near incessant singing both by day and by night. Now silence.

Other mockingbirds in the broad neighborhood are similarly silent today, as though they all received the same message. Their reproductive season is at an end, and they all know it, all at once. Quite amazing!

Kites.

Walking the dog in early morning I catch a glimpse of movement on the horizon, through and just above the treetops. The impression is of powerful, bounding, buoyant flight. "Mississippi kite," I immediately think. Then searching that part of the sky for a few moments, I get a good look. A light gray hawklike bird; long wings coming to a point at the tips; long, square-tipped tail of darker gray; throat of lighter gray, almost white: A Mississippi kite, maybe the best flyer in America!

I have watched these birds for minutes at a time, following their movements with binoculars for as long as I could keep them in view. Drastically changing directions in an instant, capable of filling the full range of rotation surrounding the air they occupy at any instant. Diving with breath-taking steepness and swiftness. As quickly converting dive into a swift sweep upward. Soaring through wide arcs across the sky employing only slight adjustments in the positioning of wings and tail.

You can sometimes see families of kites out together at this time of summer and watch the youngsters going through their paces, practicing all manner of amazing flight patterns and adjustments. How marvelous must be the experience of the birds in discovering the range and depth of their mastery of the air! What utter pleasure they must encounter at the accomplishment of masterful flight! I speculate about the birds' experiences but can be certain of mine in watching them.

These birds earn their living chiefly by snatching flying insects—often quite large ones like cicadas and dragonflies—out of the air. They are superbly suited to the job. They are a spectacular illustration of the high degree of perfection achievable by time and evolution. They are a vivid example of the beauty of nature. I recall a statement by the philosopher, Leibniz, that, when I read it, I immediately applied to the idea of evolution, though I suspect Leibniz had creation in general in mind rather than evolution in particular. It went something like this: "It seems clear to expect that when God went about His creation He would have used the simplest and most elegant possible means of accomplishing the desired work." I find that illustrated by what I know of evolution, and by what I know of Mississippi kites.

The Light of Autumn.

Today is August 7, and this morning for the first time this year I noticed the Light in August, as memorialized in Faulkner's title by that name. Light in August is the beginning of the light of autumn. Something to do with the slanting of the light, with the angle of the Earth in its tilt versus the Sun. The light becomes more golden and acquires a purer quality. I noticed it first this morning in the reflection of light from the slick and shiny surfaces of the leaves of a black gum tree. An extra golden quality in the yellow-white light coming off the leaves. Looking up among them I could see that a few had already turned that deep and brilliant shade of turkey red that they all assume in autumn. Later in the day, as I walked Pilot in one of the city parks nearby, I remarked, again, the light of August in the sun-spangled woods along the creek, in the stark contrast of dark shade and bright golden spots of sunshine.

In the Ghost River scenic area, a few miles from home in Tennessee. Late August light seems to glow from within the trees of the woods and from within the duckweed covering much of the surface of the water in the tupelo-gum swamp. The air is air is fresh and dry, only slightly warm.

> Cicadas singing
> Deep within the swamp,
> In ambient light.

By mid-November the light has started to pale; the shortening of the days has become noticeable on a daily basis. The low ebb is nearing, and winter is on its way.

Early Cooling.

Blessed spell of cool weather in mid–August. Good breezes. Low seventies at daybreak. Comfort through the early morning for walking. We see a spotted sandpiper at the lakes in City Park, a migrant from far to the north. Large numbers of blackbirds are trading the skies of morning. Earlier migrants I had seen were all swallows, particularly large numbers of purple martins, who finish their breeding activities so early, then head south.

The semi–domestic ducks and geese of the park assume a closer semblance to their fully wild cousins on early cool mornings. Mallards dabbling in the shallows as they should. They look like real birds again. We watched and listened as a group of a dozen Canadas flew straight toward us, talking among themselves incessantly, as they always do when flying. As they came just in front of us a large bird out toward the left side of the formation quickly pointed his long neck out to the left and gave an extended and prolonged call, then cut sharply to his left and set his wings in a glide. The other birds in the flock immediately made the same adjustment and they followed the leader down to land at the middle of an athletic field, where they began at once to feed on the green grass.

The walnut tree in the back yard already looks like fall, many of its leaves are yellow and a good many already have fallen. It matches one of the sweet gums in the neighborhood with half its leaves yellow and many already on the ground. Squirrels have been working over the crop on one of the pecans in the front yard. The grass beneath its limbs is littered with their cuttings so that it crunches when you walk there. The pecans still are covered with their thick green husks, but the squirrels bite big chunks out of the husks and get at the still unripe pecan meats within—these would be far too stringent for you or me, but the squirrels find them quite pleasing.

Cathy and I took Pilot to Chewalla Lake over in the mountain country past Holly Springs and let him go for a long walk through the open woods above the lake. He was so moved by the many new smells that he approached the point of over-excitement as he darted from one place to another as though there were nowhere nearly enough time to see what he needed to see and smell what he needed to smell. The terrain around the lake reminded me of the New Mexico high country, as it always does. And already, there is an autumn look to these woods, as well.

Old Bird in Town.

A few minutes ago Cathy and I saw a Cooper's hawk right in the old town square of Olive Branch. I was driving through traffic and Cathy spotted it. She could hardly believe it was really a hawk right there in the center of town—and sitting atop the front edge of the building that had been my grandfather's general store nearly a hundred years ago. This was a male Cooper's hawk, the bird known widely and with keen respect as the feared Blue Darter, notorious chicken-killer. It was said the Darter could dive into a chicken yard, grab a hen, and be gone into the timber before a farmer standing in wait with shotgun in hand could get off a shot at it. There were people walking by on the street below and motorized traffic on several sides, but the Darter in this instance took no concern for them. Rather it held its wings partly open and fanned its striped tail to half spread as it stared intently at the roof edge to its side. I suspect it had spotted sparrows on the roof and maybe had seen one go into hiding somewhere along the edge.

It occurred to me that the scene, as far as the hawk was concerned, could just as well been taking place in the year 1924 as now, and could just as well have been witnessed by a couple of boys who were my Uncle Mack and my father as by Cathy and me. Maybe the boys would have been playing baseball in the open field across the Goodman Road from their father's store. The Cooper's hawk, the very essence of wildness now, as then, might as well have been the same bird.

Terrain.

High Country.

It's widely understood that altitude is one of the main determiners of local climate: Going higher equals moving north. Entire communities of plant-life change as we move upward on a single mountain. Changes in plant communities, as well as differences in temperature, colder the higher we go, promote different communities of birds and mammals. This is demonstrated impressively to anyone who has traveled widely in the high country of the West and then travels from the South up to the northern parts of New York state or to Maine. The trees change as you move north until you arrive at tree communities that resemble those of the high Rocky Mountains, with many corresponding changes in the bird and mammal inhabitants of the area.

Nothing compares with traveling from the heat and humidity of a Southern July out to the Rocky Mountains and up the slope to at least eighty-five hundred feet altitude. The air is cool, the streams are clear and cold, the humidity is low, the light is striking, and the visual appearance of every individual aspect of the landscape is more vivid and dramatic. The bird population is almost entirely different, almost all new to a bird enthusiast who has never before traveled west.

Some of the same changes can be experienced by heading from low country to the mountains of the East. You usually reach lower temperatures—quite welcome in summer—and you arrive at new groups of plants and find some new birds and mammals. The changes are not as dramatic as those encountered in the western mountains, but they come close in regard to the trees and streams. The amount of decrease in humidity is not nearly as great as in the West and, correspondingly, the enhanced sharpness and beauty of visual objects is not nearly so dramatic.

The enhanced visual esthetics of the West are not limited to the high mountains but are the benefit of low humidity characteristic of inland country in the West at all altitudes. Objects in the low country of Big Bend National Park shine with the same clarity and vividness as they do in the high Chisos Mountains.

One of the visual treats available in the West is a view of the stars at night. Anywhere that is free of light pollution, as much of the West is, affords a striking view of the night sky that is rarely available in the East. I readily recall the vividness and brightness of the stars of the Eagle, *Aquilla*, in the August sky of Colorado.

The Wet and the Dry.

In the Rocky Mountains there's often a dry side and a wet side to mountain ranges, particularly those that trend to a north-south direction in their axes. Louis L'Amour once titled a novel *Over on the Dry Side,* about a man who had built his cabin high up on the dry side of the range, at a place where he could gaze daily on distance.

The typical movement of weather systems from west to east, and the effect of the rapid altitude gain demanded as the systems traverse a mountain range, provide for dry side / wet side conditions. As a group of moisture laden clouds is pushed across a mountain range, it is forced ever higher by the rising elevation of the land, and often it is not until the rise has neared or reached its maximum height that conditions are met for the condensation of the clouds' moisture into rain. Thus the clouds may cross over much of the west side of a range without losing much of their moisture, then have it knocked out at the top of the range. Rain begins to fall then and continues to fall for a while as the system moves on toward the east, still at the high elevation it achieved in climbing above the mountains.

The dry side is comparatively wide open, with sparse and separated vegetation; sweeping, far-ranging views open on every side. There's more desert-like vegetation, more desert birds and animals, more pine and less deciduous timber. More striking streams standing in obvious contrast to the dry country stretching away from their banks.

The wet side, by contrast is rich and lush in plant growth. Lots of spruce and fir, plenty of aspen and alder. Birds and mammals that favor moisture-rich forest. Plenty of grass that looks so full of moisture it must be good eating. You're tempted to try a bite, yourself.

Lots of wild rose and moss. Lush, full streams with wet, moisture rich banks. Good trout fishing. The happy combination of land and plant-life that, particularly at elevations of eight to nine thousand feet, provides inspiration for the descriptive phrase *fat country*.

Desert, The Big Bend.

The big bend of the Rio Grande River in Southwest Texas is a marvelous country of mountains, grasslands, and desert. It is a dry country. The driest areas are desert. Where there is a little more water, the cactus and other desert plants are accompanied by a decent growth of grass, and in some places, grasses cover much of the hillsides. In the high mountains there's been enough moisture knocked out of the clouds by elevation to afford a generous growth of forest. It's mostly coniferous forest and much of it pinyon and juniper on the lower levels, trending to ponderosa pine and finally Douglas fir as you go up. In the higher reaches of the Chisos Mountains there's even some growth of aspens.

The lower elevations of Big Bend National Park are pure Sonoran desert. Much of the area resembles a huge and meticulously arranged rock garden, perfectly supplied with a wide variety of attractive but decidedly hardy and prickly plants. There's a scattered growth of grass here and there among numerous sizes, shapes, and styles of cactus. Many of the cactuses have showy flowers, if you catch them at the right time. There's an abundance of the lowly creosote brush and a variety of deciduous brush scattered about, especially where occasional run-off of water along a wash has provided a slight increase in available moisture. Along the few permanent streams, such as the Rio Grande, is found the graceful tamarask.

A great number of animals thrive in the Sonoran desert. All manner of insects, reptiles, birds, and mammals wander the garden. Both the white-tailed and the mule deer are found in the park, but the white-tailed variety confines itself to the high country of the Chisos while the mule deer range widely across the desert. Coyotes are abundant and often seen. I'm sure bobcats are abundant, too, but they are rarely seen. This park contains one of the wildest stretches of country to be found in the southern half of North America, and I'm sure there are a proper number of lions inhabiting it, making use of the populous deer herd, but regrettably, I've never seen one. There are lots of desert specialties, as well as Mexican specialties, among the birdlife. Probably the best birds I've found here have been the zone-tailed hawk, the gray vireo, and the varied bunting. I have to mention the peregrine falcon, as well. I found them nesting in the high-up cliffs of Santa Elena Canyon at a time when they had become much rarer than they are today, before they recovered so well from the ravages of the pesticide DDT.

There are many permanent water sources scattered about the desert, and any and all of them are magnets and central destinations of animal activity. This is especially true of highly localized springs and water holes. Their resources are not spread widely across miles of country, like the River, but are centered in a single, limited area, making it a hub, a virtual beehive of action. With a park map and a four-wheeled drive jeep you can get to a great many such places. They are always worth the visit and a bit of wait to see what birds, mammals, and other animal life will make their appearance.

Favorite views in the Big Bend park: Sotol Overlook, looking back down a thousand feet, over the graceful pointed bayonets of sotol leaves, across five miles of desert to the tall cleft in the Mesa of Angels that is Santa Elena Canyon; Green Gulch, a broad hollow, or gulch, leading from the lower desert up to the entrance of the high country of the Chisos Mountains, colorful and green with plant life despite its desert dryness; the Chisos Basin, spectacular mountain amphitheater, the tall rectangular block of Casa Grande Peak dominating the view to the northeast and that wedge in the encircling wall of mountains called The Window opening the view far down into the lower desert on the southwest; and Boot Springs, an oasis of 'fat country' near the top of the Chisos, where I found the rare Colima Warbler in breeding season.

Hill and valley.

I grew up in the hill country of North Mississippi, and it is there that both sets of my great grandparents on my father's side were born. The town of Olive Branch, half a day's horseback ride south of Memphis, grew up along the broad top of a long ridge running roughly north and south. The ridge rises only forty or fifty feet from the lower land on either side and is so wide across its top that I was well up in years before I realized how completely the town was located atop a ridge. I remember how strange it seemed to us when a visiting team of baseball players from a town well out in the flat delta of the Mississippi River were so impressed by how hilly it is in our part of the state. To them, it seemed almost mountainous.

A favorite section of hill and valley country for me lies in north central Mississippi around the town of Ashland and southward along the Tippah River to Potts Camp. Many of the hills there are eighty to one hundred feet high and lined by clean, wide valleys that often have a stream running through at the bottom. Many of these valleys contain floors that have been leveled and built up in topsoil by the overflow of the valley's stream hundreds of times over past millennia. I've heard it said that the topsoil of the Mississippi delta around the town of Greenville is forty feet deep. The alluvial plains of these smaller streams don't rival the topsoil depth of the Mississippi delta, yet they have provided fine farming ground for the families who settled these hills and thrived here. When I was growing up our family farmed a piece of alluvial land on either side of Lick Creek in east Olive Branch. My grandmother prized that piece and called it 'the delta land.'

As one nears Ashland, the country becomes almost frankly mountainous, and that landscape continues down through the town of Blue Mountain, where a small college has operated for over a hundred years, and on southward through Holly Springs and Oxford. The deciduous forest is lush through much of this country, and the native short-leafed pines give it a Western look. Thacker's Mountain outside Oxford is one of the highest elevations in the central part of the state at nearly seven hundred feet. Higher ground in Mississippi can be found in the northeastern corner, where the Cumberland Plateau of north Alabama reaches into our state around the site of Tishamingo State Park, a truly beautiful place and in every way a mountain park. Bear Creek, running through the valley there, is one of the prettiest streams in the state.

There is beautiful hill and valley all across the country, though one usually associates it much more with the eastern half than the western. In the West we think of foot hills mostly running to mountains. In the East the mountains aren't nearly so high and often are more like hills. A particularly attractive section of hill country is the landscape of middle Tennessee between the cities of Clarkeville in the north and Nashville in the center. Many of the hilltops are higher than one hundred feet above their valleys. Most are almost clear of timber and covered with lush meadow. The valley bottoms are drained by clear, chuckling streams and timbered in thriving hardwoods, with much maple and scarlet oak, their leaves shining in summer with healthy green and in fall with glowing red.

Once when Cathy and I were driving through a gap high between tall ridges in eastern Tennessee, we saw a wild turkey take flight from near the top of the hill on the north ridge and fly, mostly gliding, straight across the width of the valley to a spot similarly high up the hill on the southern side of the valley. Now, I've seen turkeys fly many times, but usually—if not always—it has been associated with a quick removal of the turkey to some place much farther away from what could have been perceived as a potential predator. Otherwise, my idea was that a turkey usually walks where it goes. But here was a turkey who used territory near the tops of two ridges on the opposite sides of a deep valley. To go from one side to the other by walking would involve traversing a great deal of forest all the way down the ridge, across the valley through some open country at the bottom, then all the way up the ridge to near the top on the other side. Much easier and more efficient to hit a glide from the north side and slide through the air over to the selected spot on the south side, which is what our turkey had just done.

> A turkey's long glide,
> One ridge-line to another
> Across the valley.

Autumn.

Best Day There Is.
First cool day of fall this year on September 9. Temp in the fifties at sun-up. Spectacular gold slanting straight across the broad horizon to strike the tree tops and shining in reflection to light the surrounding world in a yellow glow. And it is yellow, all right, not white, yellow as butter. I've compared it directly with the white blossoms of crepe myrtles that fringe our front porch. The difference is plain.

The gold quality of the light lasts all this day—that light of autumn that begins in August and strengthens through October.

> Yellow as butter.
> It's the light of September,
> Following August.

Robins in numbers chirped lively and loudly across the neighborhood in early morning. They're among the first that have been here since the residents finished the year's nesting and dispersed away. Their absence was more pronounced than it often is, I think, because of the extended dry spell we had this summer. I wonder if their breeding was anywhere nearly as successful as usual. The dry conditions would seem to make it tough for a good worm harvest and well-fed baby robins. The chirping robins were soon joined and then dominated by the cheery singing of the reigning male wren who, as he often does, surprises everyone by the volume of song he achieves.

Colorado September.

We walked up the long hill along the edge of the forest of fir and aspen, with a broad meadow to our left stretching more than half a mile to the forest on the other side of the hill and reaching downhill from there over a mile to the bank of the Rio Grande. We were well out from town, but there was a good dirt road running down to a launching spot on the river, and there were a couple of vehicles down there next to the water. The meadow was grown tall with grass from the forest at each side and at the top of the hill all the way down to the river. The grass shone gold like ripe wheat in full sunshine. The sky was free of clouds and running clear and deep with that cobalt blue you never can see often enough, and then, only in the high mountains.

A group of mountain chickadees kept us lively company part of the way up and we saw one of the dark woodpeckers of the mountain forest, a sapsucker, feeding low along the trunk of an aspen, and then flying leisurely away deeper into the forest. We sat long at the top of the meadow facing down the slope to the river in the distance. The colors of the sky and the long grass, yellow aspens, and dark green firs in full sunlight were more than spectacular. They were living perfection. It was almost painful, heart-breaking to experience them so vividly. Because you wanted more. You wanted to become one with them, simply to exist with them.

The bounty of autumn was before us and around us as walked leisurely halfway down the long hill to where our truck was parked. We drove slowly down the two-wheel track to where it entered the dirt road connecting with the river and went on down to the river's edge and walked the bank for a while, taking in the magnificent views available wherever we should turn our eyes. The afternoon lasted a long time, but it couldn't last long enough. It was the kind of time you don't want to leave.

But I will see it all again someday, in a perfect autumn.

In a Range Far Away.

In a range far away
Where the sounds through the day
Are unchanged by the passage of years,
The grizzly holds sway
And the chickarees play
And the elk herd at evening appears.

The gray rock soars high
From a stream to the sky
At the edge of a high-mountain vale,

And tall grasses sway
As a breeze makes its way
Down a long slope that climbs from the shale.

Clark's nutcrackers trade
From the ridge to the glade
As the mornings stretch into a noon.
Grasshoppers parade
Through the sun and the shade
Till the late-evening rise of the moon.

Coyote mates howl
In the midst of a prowl
From the trees to the edge of the stream,
Then search through the grass,
Ears alert for the pass
Of a mouse or a vole down a seam.

Quaking aspens and firs
Ripple when the air stirs
Along a high ridge near the line;
And below on broad benches
The full sunshine drenches
Great forests of fat yellow pine.

On a path through these trees
Beside rocky debris
Is the spot where a lion killed a deer.
It was on a dark night,
The cat springing to flight
From a branch near the edge of the clear.

Many nights in mid–May
With the moon bright as day
A great-horned owl called for his mate,
And she flew to his side
And behaved as his bride
Their fierce-rising hunger to sate.

And the pair raised a brood
In the depths of the wood
Till the young ones grew strong and mature,
Then left them alone
To get by on their own
In a freedom unfettered and pure.

Once at dusk a great bear
Hid beside pasture fair
To ambush the elk when they came.
Casting far back his sight
He remembered the night,
As a cub, when his dam did the same.

Long he waited concealed
Till the herd was revealed
Till they stood just beyond a long jump.
Then he leapt fast as thought,
And a young cow was caught,
And her head twisted over her rump.

And the bear strolled that night
With the heavens alight
From the glow of the great Milky Way.

A new moon in the west
Lighted snow on the crest
And his coat shone a silvery gray.

It is said we must fly
To the light when we die
To the source of the universe made.
As for me, I would hie—
When the time comes to fly—
To that pure light that shines in the glade.

Early Fall in the Delta.

Cypress trees are turning red along the bayous and there is a yellow tint in the elms and catalpa trees. Fall flowers are coming out. Clouds of white snakeroot and goldenrod float above the grass fields. A broad flat that was underwater much of the summer is festooned in bright yellow daisies (sticktights). Rose mallows of late summer are reaching their maximum bloom. Morning glories are widespread, as are the orange blooms of trumpet vine. Tall purple thistles are plentiful, and the tough but modest ironweeds are out with purple blossoms. The humble bitterweed, bane of our home milk production when I was a child and its foliage became cattle feed and from there became an unwanted taste in our milk, continues its long blooming season past the final days of summer.

Fall Campaign.

Mockingbird started singing again this morning just before ten o'clock—his first songs since July, when he ended his breeding season. Beginning again, he delivers his songs at low volume and with extended pauses between phrases, as if in a relaxed mode. But he is back on the job, taking the ownership of his territory into the fall season, preparing to hold it through the winter in readiness for next year's breeding.

Later in the day I heard other mockingbirds through-out the broader area as they began to sing from their territories, maybe some were responding to the songs of our Mockingbird, but more likely they were reacting to the same conditions—both physiological and environ-mental—that had inspired the Yard Boss to action.

The Boss also began another behavior I had not seen for a number of weeks—that of extending his wings in two distinct movements until they are fully spread. He does this as he patrols the lawn as thought on the alert for insects to catch. And it's possible the display could startle a hidden insect into movement. But what it also does is to flash a prominent mockingbird field sign across the territory by revealing the big white patches on the backs of the wings. The display may alert any rivals nearby than the territory is taken and will be defended against intrusion. The reappearance of the behavior in time with the beginning of fall singing leads me to believe it is more a territorial display than a feeding technique.

Soft air and stillness,
Walnuts hang without motion.
A mockingbird speaks.

Hatchie Wildlife Reserve, West Tennessee.

O'Neal Lake showed in reflection a deeper blue than the sky above. Wild flowers covered the fields at the edges of the lake. Two species of daisies, snakeroot, and golden rod. Green herons in migration flushed from their hiding places all around the edges of the lake as we travelled around it. (I knew they were migrating birds because there were far too many present to have spent the summer season in one limited stretch of habitat.) A tight group of more than a dozen teal zipped out of the high sky and skated above the waters of the lake, banked sharply side-on to us so that the sun behind us shone directly on the sky blue of their wing patches. After that, a migrating shorebird called a yellowlegs (for obvious reasons) came low over the lake and landed near the far edge.

Butterflies were numerous all around the lake, dozens upon dozens upon dozens. Viceroys, red admirals, swallowtails, some small species I didn't identify, and hundreds of cloudless sulfurs—harbingers of the season.

> In pools of sunlight
> Butterflies yellow as leaves
> Who only live now.

In the San Juan Mountains.

Cathy and I drove back from the Last Dollar Road past Mt. Sneffles to a cafe in Ridgeway, Colorado to eat lunch. There were posters around the walls of John Wayne and cast members of the movie *True Grit*. Most of the town scenes in that movie were filmed here in Ridgeway and the back-country scenes were filmed in sections of the San Juan National Forest in the surrounding area. Many of these took place off the Owl Creek Pass Road where Cathy and I were headed this afternoon.

The road passed through fine ranch land and along and across perfect mountain streams. To the east and swinging toward the south were the rugged cliff edges of the Uncompahgre Plateau, with impressive peaks and hobgoblin boulders. The road was of gravel but was good, and double-track wide all the way to the pass. About halfway up you come onto the mountain proper among forests of aspen and fir.

The aspens were in good color, shining yellow-gold, and the day was fair, warm, and sunny. At a big curve in the road way up near the pass I was utterly surprised to recognize the open meadow where marshal Rooster Cogburn made his one-man cavalry charge against the Lucky Ned Pepper gang in the movie.

The place was surrounded by big aspens along the edges of the meadow and gave open views of high peaks and ranges in the distance. This is the scene where John Wayne takes the reins in his teeth and goes in firing with a gun in each hand. I easily recognized the place from the pictures in the movie, but it was smaller in real life than it had appeared on film. I realized with fresh appreciation how much is controlled by selecting camera angles, how things are framed, and times of the day for filming. It was a revelation of the degree to which movie makers *create* the world they present.

We went on through the forest right up to the

top of the pass and had a view down the other side through a valley framing a great mass of rock mountain standing clean and tall above timberline. Dense forest stretched down and out toward the base of the peak in the distance. The good weather held all afternoon, and you couldn't have invented a better day.

Not only Cathy and I and our children, but all my brothers and their children have loved the Rocky Mountains over the years, and many times we have been able to spend summer days and nights camping there in a family group. Most of the males in the group would rise every morning before the sun came up. It was so cold you didn't want to sit down, and we would stand in single line facing East, clutching cups of hot coffee.

> Cold in the shadow
> Of the high mountain valley,
> Awaiting the sun.

Green River Overlook, Canyonlands National Park.

The startling, sweeping view is wide open across vast distance down the great width of the river canyon. The gravitational voltage almost pulls you toward that yawning, awe-inspiring space, toward the canyon floor and the Green River thousands of feet directly below. You feel you could fly through that space, for a time, and come to union with a palpable elemental presence, and I suppose you could. You know you won't do it, but you won't deny the pull. It makes you step back a little farther from the rim. The massive structure of the canyon stands before the eye at a single look; sheer rock walls dropping in tiers all the way to the river and outward toward the edge of infinity.

I first saw this view on an evening many years ago when Cathy and I brought the children to camp here. There was no one but us in the area that night, and it was long before the government erected a restraining fence to prevent foolish visitors from plunging over the edge to certain death. I approached the edge alone and tucked my head and lowered the bill of my cap so I could creep up to the rim without seeing the approaching view. As I saw the toes of my boots nearing the edge, I lifted my head in a quick move to take in the scene at full strength and at one blow. It took my breath, as though I had been struck in the stomach; I literally gasped, didn't return to regular breathing for good number of seconds.

> At the edge of Earth!
> Sudden punch of gravity,
> Shocking reach of space.

A Day's Welcome.

Morning sunshine pooling across the yard. Cut it with a knife if you like. Mockingbird song across the neighborhood. I see three territorial disputes within a short time, each involving a number of different mockingbirds. Young birds of the summer's production are seeking their own niches within a zone where most suitable territory is already taken.

Yard Boss was chief actor in one of these disputes, easily rousting a group of three trespassers from his domain. It took him twenty seconds. I don't doubt he enjoyed it immensely. The youngsters seemed to possess few clues as to what they were about, nearly helpless before the onslaught of an old pro. The old pro, vigorous and supremely confident. The Yard Boss.

The air fairly snaps with excitement, quickening your breath, provoking deep inhalation, lifting spirits in an immediate ascent. Genuine chill in the air. Nothing like summer out here today. No morning like this has hit Mississippi since April.

Sunlight pours into the yard from the west in late afternoon. A big hatch of flying insects swarms through the shafts of light. Good news, if we had a trout stream in the yard. But these were tiny insects. We have no artificial flies anywhere nearly this small. Even if we had the stream, we couldn't match the real bait. But it's still true, as I've often repeated to myself and others: If you're going to have weather like this, you may as well be in the Rocky Mountains. The weather brings the mountains to Mississippi if you wait long enough and keep alert. Fall arrived today in strength. Welcome. Welcome, indeed, my old and excellent friend.

> Morning spread slowly
> Along the ridge and the lake—
> Nothing much happened.

October Morning.

The white birds, American egrets, gathered at a clear, shallow pond of fresh water a mile or so back from the Gulf of Mexico. They were surrounded for a great distance on all sides by a smooth plain studded with palmetto and numerous patches of green grass. The area had sustained a serious burn the past year. Most of the large bushes had perished in the fire and were gone, leaving the broad expanse attractively clean and open. Half a mile north of the birds rose the first ridge of the Alabama mainland, covered with live oaks and pines.

From their location in the open plain, the birds would see the approach of a potential enemy from far away and would have the leisure of time to react appropriately. They were tall birds, and graceful in their movements, particularly those by which they approached the attack of their prey of small aquatic animals. Their strikes were swift and sure and almost never missed. They came to the alert many more times than they struck, withholding the strike until the chance of success was great.

The brilliant white of the birds struck vividly across the distance in the bright sunlight of morning. From time to time, one or another of them would lift into the air and fly a short distance to change its watching and hunting post. The light from their wing movements flashed through the crystal air.

The Eagle.

From its perch on a mountain ledge nearly a mile away, the golden eagle had spotted a marmot as it emerged from its den on the slope of a peak in the near distance. The spectacular vision of the eagle was capable not only of sensing the movement so far away but of identifying features that matched those of a well formed hunting-image long ago retained in his memory storage. He didn't know the word *marmot*, of course, not that nor any other word. Yet he readily brought to consciousness the image of a marmot, recognized it as a fine food item often used before, recalled the types of attacks that had been effective against it in the past, and even anticipated the feel of grasping the rather large sized animal in his talons. Without further processing he sprang from his perch and began a long glide toward the marmot, well away and more than a thousand feet below the eagle's altitude.

The marmot stepped out into the warm sun of late afternoon and stretched himself luxuriously near the mouth of his den. He had searched and watched the surrounding skies and nearby slopes for a considerable time before leaving the safety of the den, and he had seen nothing to cause him concern. Nevertheless, he was ready to dive back into the den at the first sign of trouble. Then he detected a movement in the sky to the west that triggered an immediate alarm. He sprang back into the mouth of the den, then turned to look back from his now safe position. He saw the eagle land at the edge of the tall cliff across from his den. The eagle remained perched there in a watchful pose.

Just as the eagle had been about to go into a steep dive on the marmot, he had seen the marmot make a dash back to its den and disappear. This had happened many times before. Usually the marmot would remain out of sight for a long time, and often in the past the eagle had given up and moved on to find other prey. But sometimes a marmot had come back out of its den as the eagle had waited. Sometimes he had caught marmots that did that. So he took a perch at the edge of a cliff and watched the mouth of the den.

For more than ten years past the eagle and his mate had maintained a nesting territory in the dry mountain and mesa country of northwestern Colorado. The country was wide open for the most part, and ideal for the hunting of golden eagles. Ever since their first season together the eagle and his mate had returned to the same territory in the very early spring of the next year, had re-established their mated status, and had begun preparations for another nesting season.

Often the pair were apart from each other during the autumn and winter as they wandered widely across the mountain country of the West from Montana to Arizona and New Mexico to Utah. By living alone at these times, the pair had the advantage that there was only one of them to feed, and each could get its own food by hunting territory that was being used by only one eagle at a time. That made a difference in some years when hard times came and food was scarce.

But they returned to the old territory with each nesting season, carried on their courtship acrobatics once more and again become mates. Each year, they added to one of their nests of previous years until the structures became huge mansions of nests. But the extra room cost them nothing and served them well. Unlike many of their species, this pair often produced two eggs within a short enough time of each other, and incubated them almost at so nearly the same time, that the two chicks were hatched almost together and were almost the same age, giving the second-hatched chick nearly as good a chance of surviving as the first-hatched had. The eagle pair had held a fortunate hunting territory through the years and were good providers, and in most of their breeding years they had produced two new adult eagles by the end of the season.

The eagle pair had two different nesting sites several miles apart within the same large territory. Some years they used one site and other years the other. The arrangement allowed them to lay claim to a widespread territory by occupying both nest sites at the beginning of each year. It ensured there would be no other eagles competing with them to rear chicks within a broad area of country and further, protected against any year-to-year carryover effects of potential over use of the country immediately surrounding either nest site.

But then, a year and a half ago, his mate had failed to return to the old territory. He had looked for her repeatedly at both of their old nest sites, but she had not appeared. He waited on the territory until the breeding season was well over half gone, then he began to wander as he had in past summers. But something was different. Some old feeling of being riveted by the unfolding events of the day was missing. A sense he had always had of the importance of his life was gone. He drifted through the days, and as late winter came and the tide of the year began to turn toward spring again, he found himself back at his old mating ground. He visited the old nest sites often and was inspirited to be back at the scenes where his life had been consuming and exciting, where the achievements of the weeks could be seen in the growth of his offspring. Where he had lived in contentment with his mate for so many seasons. But again, she was not there. She did not arrive. There were no chicks, anymore. So one day he just drifted away and was gone.

He had no interest in breeding, now. Or much interest in anything else. Even the pleasure he had always taken in flight was missing now from his life. The excitement he had taken in attacking his prey was missing, as well, and even when he made a kill, often he was not much interested in eating.

As he sat now on the ledge above the marmot's den, he gradually lost focus on the possibility of seeing the marmot again. He wanted no food now, anyway, had little interest in launching an attack. At a certain moment, he felt his feet began to lose their hold on the rocks at the cliff's edge and felt his body begin to pitch forward into the void.

At first it appeared the eagle had launched itself in an attack, and the marmot clung tighter to the edge of its den, ready to dart backward and out of reach. But there was something peculiar about the eagle's posture. There was no strength in it. The wings hung listlessly at the bird's sides. Then the eagle turned in a somersault and crashed on its back into the shale at the base of the cliff. Its body bounced slightly as it landed.

And the eagle... It was almost like dreaming. Quiet, with just the whisper of the wind; drifting above mesas and mountain tops incredibly far below; afloat on the moving air, newly found strength and joy, effortless lift beneath the wings, happiness, freedom, gliding on, and on. Then in the distance, the form of another large bird moving along before him on the same course. As he watched, the bird flared its wings aslant and veered about to head directly toward him. And he recognized her immediately. It was his mate. He had found her once again.

October Woods.

The big woods in early morning: Smell of oak leaves fallen to the ground, dried for days, then moistened in heavy dew. The dense fog of dawn clears in the growing strength of the rising sun. Golden light suffuses bright leaves. The air sings.

Rainy Day in Fall.

After dark the rain came in a heavy curtain, a rate of four inches per hour. Presently the rate declined, but the rain continued long through the night, with occasional heavy single booms of lightning. Morning came in heavy and gray as mid-winter; rain continued in pale light.

Maybe this moisture will extend the life of deciduous leaves and provide more color into the advance of the season. But it comes at the loss of two days of the weather you look forward to through all the rest of the year.

Another day, the rain has gone. The sun is back, brighter than hope. Easy wind in a steady flow form the west. Air dry and cool. October is back. Ode to Joy.

Letter from the Past.

The old graveyard stood gracefully in the bright afternoon sun. Huge post oaks cast deep shade upon the edges of the meadow. Near the center of the lawn, just a few steps apart from one another, two small groupings of monuments represent immediate ancestors—both maternal and paternal—from my father's side of the family. On the right side, the Haraways; on the left, the McNeills.

Achilles Momen Haraway, the patriarch of my grandfather's side of the family, was born in Virginia in 1814 and died at Center Hill on September 11, 1891. His wife of fifty-five years, my great-great grandmother Julia McCargo Haraway, died one week later. Family tradition says she died of a broken heart.

Their son, my great-grandfather, David Herndon Haraway served in the 34th Mississippi infantry in the Civil War. We have one surviving letter he wrote to his wife, Martha McGowan Haraway, from Lookout Mountain, Tennessee before the battles of Lookout Mountain, Missionary Ridge, and Chickamauga. Here is a little of what he wrote back to "Mattie."

My dear little wife it is with the greatest pleasure that I am permitted to write you a few lines to answer your very interesting letters which I received yesterday on picket and was rejoiced to hear from you and that you are doing so well and enjoying yourself so well and to thank you for sending me my cap. It came in good time—I slept in it last night and it kept my head as warm as you please.. . ..

I like to have forgot to tell you about the cape you spoke of that you said you were going to Memphis after it if you could not get anyone else to go. I told you about going to Memphis and if your Aunt and Mollie want to see you they can come out to Pa's. I don't want you to go to Memphis and I had rather stay wet and do without a cape 100 years than for you to go to Memphis, I don't want you to go.. . . Oh! You said you would like to hear me say that I love you, I can't say it but I can write it. I do love you more than anything else on earth. I wish you were here about an hour to see the beautiful mountains and the 2 armies so close to each other, but I would want you away from here very quick.. . .

Give my respects to Mr. Barringer and family and to all inquiring friends. Accept my love for your own sweet little self. Write soon and as often as you can. Your true and devoted husband,

Old Dave

Dave survived the war in good health and returned to live with Mattie at Center Hill for forty-six more years.

Autumn Evening.

At the last of day the sun hit the trees as it does in the Rocky Mountains. A half moon stood vertically in the sky of midnight blue above the bare limbs and hanging nuts of the walnut tree. The red planet Mars emerged from the darkening sky above the moon, and the cricket chorus welcomed the coming of night.

> Crickets and tree-frogs
> Across darkening forest,
> Begin the old songs.

Fall Afternoon in Louisiana.

The road runs down abruptly from a ridge of hills covered with mature hardwood and mixed pine timber onto open and flat bottomland stretching seventy miles east to the Mississippi River. Local sites throughout that delta that are high enough to have remained dry in even the biggest floods of modern memory have names like Waterproof and Sicily Island. Floods like that aren't supposed to happen anymore and, so far, haven't happened, since the U. S. Army Corps of Engineers threw up its levees and control structures and took over responsibility for managing the lower Mississippi River back in the 1930s. But the Mississippi is a big old powerful river; we'll just have to see.

Close against the edge of the bluff a large creek runs southward into a semi-open swamp and marsh. To the north side of the bridge over the creek a grassy marsh half a mile wide stretches out of sight along the flat-land side of the creek. On the south side is a large, slick-water swamp, with numerous dead stumps of various heights and quite a few trees that are still living. The road across the marsh and swamp from the creek bridge is built atop a wide earthen levee, with additional bridges thrown in here and there to accommodate the flow in times of high water. There are wide, graveled shoulders on each side of the road to allow parking by fishermen and duck hunters, who use the area to launch their boats for access to the marsh and the swamp.

I pulled the truck well over onto the swamp-side shoulder of the road and set up the tripod of a spotting scope in the bed of the truck, providing a raised platform from which I could look well out into the swamp. The place was empty of people. At least 2,000 ducks were feeding and resting in the near distance on the east side of the swamp. Most of them were gadwalls, but there were mallards and shovelers here and there and several large bunches of green-winged teal in close groups. As the afternoon drifted on toward sunset, more and more ducks arrived in bunches of a dozen or more, each group circling the host of birds already on the water before selecting a landing spot and abruptly and almost simultaneously assuming a long, swaying, gracefully sculpted glide down to the water—the long glide of ducks to the water from three hundred feet, one of the most beautiful actions in nature.

As the sky started to redden in the west, large flocks of blackbirds and grackles began pouring down into the stands of cypress trees lining the old creek-bed running out into the swamp. The blackbirds were quite noisy, as they often are, carrying on a constant cacophony of vocalizations that often strike me as boisterous and raucous. I can't help thinking they sound raucous to the blackbirds. Maybe in addition to providing a constant stream of information on the changing location of group members, they give the individuals of the flock a feeling of being part of a formidable group. But then, it's difficult for a person to say how a blackbird feels.

Many of the lower limbs of the trees in which the blackbirds had landed reached down to the surface of the water, and members of the flock crowded out onto these limbs in large numbers to obtain a drink before settling to roost for the night. Their roosting place this night afforded both an evening drink as well as protection from easy approach by land-based predators. And the large numbers of individuals comprising the flock afforded, as always, the presence of thousands of eyes and ears attuned to the approach of an enemy.

The conclusion of the day came on quickly. It had been suitably cool and suitably warm, had been enriched by the presence of thousands of wild birds, and now reached its finish in a fine sunset. I climbed into the truck and drove homeward through the twilight, anticipating the company of my wife.

The Woods of Autumn.

Golden light suffused the forest parkland as if the air itself had color—bright, deep, and mellow. It shone through the yellow leaves of hickory and the red leaves of dogwood and the yellows, oranges, pinks, and reds of the maples and sweet gums. Poison ivy and Virginia creeper vines added their own reds and deep pinks where they had climbed high up the trunks of trees and even into the higher limbs. Here and there a scarlet oak glowed, its leaves a deep turkey red. The afternoon was rich in harmony and peace, rich in beneficence, powerful in soul, deep in existence.

Big short-leaf pines contributed a mountain look to the woods in many places and gave the scene a flavor of the western mountains. A pair of flickers, still together in fall as they are throughout the year, hunted the open meadow of a clearing looking for insects or worms. They flew away toward the shore of the big lake just over the hill.

A mature white-tailed deer stood in the left side of the road before us as we drove out of the forest toward home. She balked at the sight of our vehicle, then reversed her direction and scampered back across the road in front of us and into the woods on the right side. As we sat unmoving in our car, a second doe came out of the woods to our left and crossed in front of us to join the first. Then, looking into the woods from which the second doe had just emerged, I saw a buck slipping away on that side. He was a good-sized buck with tall, white horns.

Falling Leaves.

High wispy clouds soften the light of afternoon, less brilliant but more mellow than before. Leaves drift in ones and twos on a gentle wafting of air from the west. A soft and deep afternoon with a temperature cool enough to make you enjoy the feel of long sleeves. A strong movement of air rustles the treetops and sets adrift dozens of leaves at once. Down they come, dozens, then hundreds. All the science now or ever will not predict where a single leaf will fall. Nor exactly when it will fall. But it is ever a graceful event. The fall of a single leaf.

> A cover of leaves
> Carpets the forest with color
> In the silent light.

Mid-November Morning.

There was frost last night and the day broke clear, windless, and cold. Birds across the neighborhood grew active as the day took hold. There was the illusion, to me, that winter had just passed and springtime was underway. The birds acted as though under the same illusion.

A titmouse repeated the territorial song of spring again and again. Jays were moving about actively from tree to tree and punctuated the moments with their loud cries. Wintering robins by the dozens spread throughout an extensive forest park looking for food of worms or insects but taking advantage, as well, of any berries they might encounter. Many of the robins, too, were singing. A large flock of grackles settled into the oak tops with the usual fanfare. Individuals communicated with the group at large by their repeated "chock, chock" vocals and, now and then, with some of their more complex, raucous, and semi-musical sounds.

Sun filled the deep-yellow canopy of a large oak, and beside it, the deep red top of a black gum. It was a morning when you might say the treetops were filled with the dancing of Blake's angels.

Science and Philosophy.

I wish, here, to pursue a logical investigation into the nature of reality. It is to be based on my own direct experiences and what I can reasonably derive from them. I wish to do this without evoking religious concepts or arguments, with one exception. The sustaining harmony and spirit I find at the center of existence is so consistent with the idea of God that I will use that name for it simply as a matter of honest word usage.

Human reason (even if based on observation) is unable take the measure of the universe, now or ever. The problem is not so much a lack of observationally based knowledge as a limitation in our power of reason. For us, everything must have a beginning. It makes no sense to say that something always *was*. Whatever now *is* must have had a beginning somewhere. On the other hand, it makes no sense to say that something could have begun from nothing.

Yet without doubt the universe is here. The situation permits two possibilities: Either the universe came from nothing or it is a continuing manifestation of something that always was, without ever having a starting point. Reason rebels at either possibility.

The problem is placed at one remove by asserting that God started the universe. The question then becomes one of where God came from. Perhaps we are more comfortable in permitting God to slip the rules of logic than we are in letting ordinary matter do the same thing. After all, God goes beyond physical existence into the realm we call the spiritual. God is at least as much spirit as he (she, it) is physical. Perhaps we will not require God to have a beginning. Nevertheless, we will have gone beyond the limitations of reason in admitting that the universe is a continuing manifestation of something, whether physical or spiritual, that always was. There is, however, a way of phrasing the latter proposition that seems less at odds with reason than any other that has occurred to me, and that is to say there really is no such thing as nothing. That is to say, *nothing never was*!

With Einstein, our scientific account of the universe began to depart from our intuitive sense of reality. Physicists began making calculations on the basis of rules describing a world far beyond that of everyday experience. They accepted the rules because they permitted accurate prediction of events that *were* open to ordinary observation—often astounding events, the like of which have never yet been derived from any other system of rules. Thus, in our science, we began to accept the idea of a universe beyond the reach of intuitive reality. This is not a temporary problem. Future advances in scientific understanding will not solve it. They will be like a light that shines farther into a tunnel, but as the light moves forward it reveals a corresponding advancement of the tunnel. Descriptions of the tunnel will continue to violate an intuitive understanding of reality.

Science is limited to a description of the observable world and derivation of principles (rules) that permit prediction and control of observable events. However complete scientific description becomes, it will never tell us what anything *means* in addition to that description. Belief in this additional meaning is the basis of religion. It is a major concern of philosophy. It is forever beyond the reach of science.

No doubt this situation is acceptable to many physicists, pleased with a system of reason-verified-by-observation that continues to reveal ever deeper recesses of the tunnel. "What is the world? Why, we learn more about the answer to that question every year." And so may we continue to do. But I suspect that some physicists, like many others of us, would welcome a final answer they can have now (while yet they live). One that will not become outdated by future discovery. One that goes beyond description to address the idea of meaning. That is the sort answer I wish to pursue here.

To say that the universe has meaning may be to say that it is imbued with spirit. At least that is consistent with my own understanding of spirit—a dimension of the world that goes beyond physical description, although it may be fully present in the physical and totally coexistent with it.

I wish to begin by asking what we can know about the meaning of the world simply by considering what surrounds us at this moment. I will address the question by applying whatever intuitive powers I can muster, including the intuitive/spiritual insight available in the sensory-like experience that followers of Zen call *satori*, and that people of spiritual insight, approaching from various religious/philosophical cultures besides Zen, have called by other names.

I would like to resolve any mystery about the experience of satori that I can, but it is a nonverbal experience that is not amenable to satisfactory verbal description. I can say that one of the direct perceptions of satori, to me, is of a living connection among the source of the universe, all things in nature, and myself. Many people have sensed a spirit-like power in the resurgent plant life of spring, in a majestic range of the Rocky Mountains, in a person's splendid behavior under difficult conditions, or in the sweep of a single human being's life. These experiences are similar in nature to satori.

But to return to the main question—after appealing to the most reliable perceptions available to me, what do I know about the universe?

1. I know the universe is filled with spirit. The spiritual is coexistent with the physical. This applies to every aspect of the universe, every detail.
2. The spirit of the universe is similar to consciousness, active awareness. There is an active transmission of awareness between the whole and its components.
3. The attitude of the whole toward its components is like that of a parent toward its children. Its respect for its components is like that of a brother for a brother.
4. One senses a single focus that encompasses all of the myriad, varied awareness in the universe. We might be tempted to call it the Eye of God, though, if we prefer, we needn't call it by a name at all.
5. Spirit/awareness was present at the beginning of the universe and expanded directly with advancement in physical development. It continues to do so, moment by moment, time without end. Incredibly rich from the beginning, it becomes richer with each

advance in the physical realization of spirit. The situation conveys rich meaning upon every realized thing. Each human life, for example, is a new thing, a new occurrence in the material realization of spirit. To illustrate, conceive if you will, that the universe (or God) was *not* advanced and honored by the football play of Johnny Unitas and Joe Montana, by the flight across the Atlantic of Lindbergh, by the writing of William Blake and William Faulkner. Imagine it, if you can. I cannot.

6. Every thing that ever was is contained within the world-focus of the present moment. As Faulkner said, "The past is never dead. In fact, it's not even past." This holds for individual people, dogs, drowned rats, and dead fleas. All are present forever in the conscious focus of the current moment.

7. There is indescribable, deep harmony at the center, in the hum and throb of world spirit. This harmony is the guardian of the universe. Nothing can stem its massive tide. It was present in power from the beginning. Its characteristics are analogous to love, happiness, wisdom, beneficence, reverence of beauty in all forms. Direct experience of—communion with—the harmony of world spirit conveys the state of mind called satori.

8. Religious *truth* is encompassed within the harmony of world spirit, but the totality of that harmony is far beyond any statement of religion, and is not itself encompassed by any collection of statements. Our best statements rise to suggestions of what exists independently as it is, independent of language, beyond language-based thinking.

I wish to address two additional questions about the metaphysics of the universe that are not answerable by appeal to direct experience (at least, not my own experience or that of anyone else of whom I have heard). Yet we can reasonably speculate about answers that are consistent with what is known by experience.

1. What was the status of God, or spirit, before the start of the physical universe? I am unable to speak with confidence on the question, but I would not care to argue that matter existed *prior* to God. The great harmony was there from the beginning. It seems comfortable to say that somehow God was there, the harmony assured, and then there was matter. What I believe we can say with full confidence is that there was no *time* prior to matter. Time, as we understand it, exists only in reference to the regular occurrence of periodic physical events—so many rotations of an electron around its nucleus, of the earth on its axis, so many trips of the earth around its orbit, so many heartbeats, or so many circuits of a minute-hand around a clock face. In the absence of time, it makes no sense to ask *how long* God may have preceded matter. (Or again, perhaps *nothing* never was.)

2. Does the universe follow the rule of absolute determinism? What is the possibility of free will in human action?

Einstein, holding for determinism, said "God does not play dice with the universe." We have said already that nothing can overthrow the massive harmony of the universe—so the whole is never at risk at a chance. But this does not necessarily mean there is absolute determinism in respect to the details of existence. Accepting Einstein's metaphor, I say that without the dice—without the possibility of free variation—the universe is meaningless. If all that happens is the unfolding of a series of events predetermined in detail from the beginning, then what is the point of the physical manifestation? There is no drama or excitement in the unfolding of a completed plan that was preordained from the start. Contrast this idea with that of a universe perpetually in the midst of *becoming*, limited only by principle guidelines—a universe in which we have responsibility in creating the character of our own lives and of influencing the world in which we act. One scenario has the lifelessness of a formula or a protocol, the other the freshness and excitement of *creation*, of God-coming-to-realized-being.

I have said above that everything that ever *was* continues forward with the expanding consciousness of God—at least insofar as it is in harmony with God's character. I am able to say that one directly encounters this state of things in the experience of satori. As Spinoza said, the brute, hardly being conscious of anything beyond his lust and greed-driven lunging, "when he ceases to struggle, ceases almost entirely to exist;" while the wise man, being conscious of the eternal character of God and of his own participation in that character, "never ceases to be, but always enjoys true peace of soul."

Robins on the Ground

It is late fall, but the same thing can happen in the South on different days through the winter and on through to late spring. Robins are here the year round, but many more are here in the winter months as we accommodate the vast numbers who venture far to the north during breeding season. After that, large groups of them travel around without noticeable schedule across the countryside of the South.

They make a bustling crowd and enliven the landscape wherever they descend from the sky to feed and to rest and, it seems, to carry on a great gossip of social interchange. They have quickened the branches of the tall cedars in my side yard, eating berries there, and spreading over to eat the bright fruits of my holly bushes while the resident mockingbird tries in vain to run them from what he views as his private preserve. The robins give way to him briefly, an individual at a time, but there are too many of them. There's no means of effective control for the mockingbird.

They often spread out across a parkland of forest and meadow, hopping vigorously about the ground gleaning whatever insects and worms they can find to eat—a robin located in every twenty or thirty foot circle for a large distance. The air is filled with their chirping calls and, now and then, one or two of their longer caroling songs. What may have seemed a drab and dull day before they arrived now is utterly changed. They have brought the countryside vividly to life.

Winter.

A Morning's Walk.

As my dog Pilot stepped around the corner of an abandoned house in an old residential neighborhood, a small hawk lifted from the grass just in front of us. I saw that it carried in its talons the body of a smaller bird. A few steps further revealed an array of red feathers, tipped in soft gray where the downy parts had lain closest to the bird's body, made it clear that the victim had been a male cardinal. The hunter undoubtedly had been a sharp-shinned hawk, a male, by its size. Sharpies are our smallest accipiters, and among this family of bird-hawks, the males are substantially smaller than the females—likely an adaptation to the female's role of guarding the young at nesting time, extra size making her a more formidable guard, while smaller size promotes efficiency of food demand in males.

The hawk flew away down a line of old trees leading toward a more dense section of old woods. As Pilot and I followed along the same line, I glimpsed the hawk two more times as it slipped away well in front of us. I saw no more of the cardinal's body. Quite possibly the hawk had already consumed it before we flushed him the second time.

This morning, about the same time as yesterday, Pilot and I again walked along the same route. To my surprise, there remained not a feather at the site of the hawk's attack. No sign at all remained of the brief life and death struggle that I knew had occurred here only a day ago.

Sharp-shin at the Door.

In mid-afternoon I notice a commotion outside the back door. A sharp-shinned hawk has chased a group of house sparrows into the heavy cover of a clump of privet hedge near the back porch. The hedge is grown over with a thick covering of honeysuckle. Both the honeysuckle and hedge have evergreen leaves, affording the sparrows a secure hiding place. The hawk sits peering into this cover, repeatedly spreading and flicking its tail in an eye-catching and strangely affecting display. Strangely affecting.

I can imagine what the display represents to any of the sparrows that see it. Even to me, the movements seem ominous and threatening. Huge danger—sudden and mortal! Get out! Get out! Escape, for God's sake! But any sparrow that breaks cover will be immediately vulnerable to the hawk. I say I can imagine these things but, in truth, the impression has occurred instantaneously and strongly with the immediacy of sensory reaction–far more rapid than rational thought.

The hawk clearly is aware of me as I stand watching from the window of the breakfast room fifteen feet away. But I am inside the house. It holds to its chance, continues to stare intently into the brush, continues to work with its tail. It changes its perch from the edge of the clump where the sparrows are hiding to the low branch of a walnut tree immediately above them and continues its tail movements and its intense gaze. The sparrows hold tight to their cover, refuse to flush or otherwise offer an opening to attack. The hawk now seems more bothered by my presence and, after another moment or two, flies away. The sparrows stay hidden (and, for now, safe).

The Clear Weather.

A crystal clear day after day upon day of gray, closed, and dreary skies. Marvelous! Heavy frost at daybreak, but the wind is down and the sun heats the air quickly. Soon the temperature is up into the forties. The dry, cool air is bracing as I take the dog for a long walk—or, he takes me. We step lively along through common scenes of town now made visually arresting by the bright light and dry air. The lines of objects stand boldly in three dimensions. The local world is far more colorful than it was earlier this same week. Evergreens...cedar and pine and holly, nandina and others stand in bold contrast to the blue sky and bright sunlight. Lawns are seen to have far more green grasses still present than suspected.

It is a fit day to be alive—a fine day to breathe and to walk and to see. Makes me think of something Thoreau said (though my recollection may miss a bit on accuracy), "By God, that ancient universe is in such fine health, I think surely it will never die."

Clear and Cold.

Cold at daybreak with a brisk north wind. Not a cloud in the sky. Later the sun is out in full strength and the day is bright as a bluebird, still cold, but not uncomfortably so. Surveying the full horizon, I find there are just three clouds across the entire visible sky. They are small clouds and widely separated, so that it seems each is sailing alone. I'm reminded of duck-hunting in midwinter forty years ago with a good friend who used to call such times in the field "bluebird days." There usually was an action-packed "fly around" time for the ducks at first light on bluebird days.

The Coldwater in Flood.

I drop off a ridge into the valley, entering a floodplain of woods and swamps on a back road near the midpoint of the river's course across Mississippi. I spot a phoebe at my first stop and stay to watch its feeding for a few minutes. It is a mid-sized flycatcher named for its call, and there are many more of them here in winter than in summer. Deeper into the swamp and closer to the river I see a great blue heron feeding at the edge of a pool and a red-shouldered watching from a hunting post in a tree well within the swamp. This a bird that loves stream-side forests and river bottoms.

In the brush and small stuff beside the road near the river, I find the first fox sparrows of the season. It's unusual to find them so early in the winter because very cold weather in the north is needed to send them this far south. They are particularly colorful sparrows that are never plentiful here. A good number of them present are present today, and they start to sing back and forth. I seldom get to hear their song because they don't breed in my part of the country. It is a pleasing and musical one, like many sparrow songs, and something about it also reminds of the songs of thrushes, the supreme masters of bird music.

A little farther across the river I spot a great number of ducks in a flooded cornfield. I drive on for a way so as not to disturb the birds, then walk back to look at them at leisure. They are all mallards. Mallards down from the north and wild as a timber wolf. They are in vigorous form, bursting with energy, delighted with the bracing air and the prospects of the flooded cornfield. They are feeding briskly, plunging their heads under and using their feet to turn their upper bodies down and hold their tails up out of the water as they stretch their long necks to search below the water's surface for food. By golly, they are called dabbling ducks, and they are dabbling now, for all they are worth. Their general vigor also finds expression in many instances of rather unseasonable courtship across the field—unseasonable as far as procreation is concerned, but I wonder if mallards recognize any time as unseasonable for courtship. Males bob their heads rapidly and repeatedly in serious flirting and many females answer with head bobs of their own.

Snowy Day.

It's been snowing on and off all day. Gray as only a snow day can be. But by mid-afternoon, the snow hasn't yet begun to accumulate. It has not been constant enough or heavy enough to build up in the windstorm that has been underway. The temperature is in the twenties and in the wind feels near zero—a killer. And it literally *would* kill you, if you stayed out in it too long. You can stay out with face uncovered only for a few minutes. Then you get in a great hurry to get back inside and under cover.

A Circle Completed.

We have finished the round of the year, have come back once more to the starting point. The Sun is coming back to accomplish again its yearly work on Earth. After a long succession of shortening days we come again to the shortest, and a corner to be turned. And I know I have come near to a corner in my own life; clearly, the shortening of my own days has arrived. But I can say truly that the prospect is not overly interesting. Rather, I look toward the coming of another spring.

I remember a song by George Harrison, the words as well as the music:

> Little darlin',
> It's been a long cold lonely winter.
> Little darlin',
> It seems like years since it's been here.
>
> Here comes the Sun.
>
> Here comes the Sun.
>
> And I say,
> It's all right.

Author's Note.

Much of the text of this book was completed in the year 2000, shortly after I retired from teaching and moved back to Mississippi. But additions and deletions were made over the ensuing years, and substantial portions were added in the year 2012.

About the Author

Maury M. Haraway is a fifth-generation native of DeSoto County, Mississippi. He received his Ph.D. from the University of Mississippi and served for many years as Professor of Psychology at the University of Louisiana, Monroe prior to retiring to his hometown of Olive Branch, where he now lives with his wife Cathy.